Improving the Software Process through Process Definition and Modeling

Improving the Software Process through Process Definition and Modeling

INTERNATIONAL THOMSON COMPUTER PRESS
I(T)P™ An International Thomson Publishing Company

London • Bonn • Boston • Johannesburg• Madrid • Melbourne • Mexico City • New York • Paris
Singapore • Tokyo • Toronto • Albany, NY • Belmont, CA • Cincinnati, OH • Detroit, MI

COPYRIGHT © 1996 International Thomson Computer Press

I(T)P˙ A division of International Thomson Publishing Inc.
The ITP logo is a trademark under license.

Printed in the United States of America

For more information, contact:

International Thomson Computer Press
20 Park Place, Suite 1001
Boston, MA 02116
USA

International Thomson Publishing
Königswinterer Strasse 418
53227 Bonn
Germany

International Thomson Publishing Europe
Berkshire House 168-173
High Holborn
London, WC1V 7AA
England

International Thomson Publishing Asia
221 Henderson Road #05-10
Henderson Building
Singapore 0315

Thomas Nelson Australia
102 Dodds Street
South Melbourne, 3205
Victoria, Australia

International Publishing Japan
Hirakawacho Kyowa Building, 3F
2-2-1 Hirakawacho
Chiyoda-ku, 102 Tokyo
Japan

Nelson Canada
1120 Birchmont Road
Scarborough, Ontario
Canada, M1K 5G4

International Thomson Editores
Campos Eliseos 385, Piso 7
Col. Polanco
11560 Mexico D. F. Mexico

International Thomson Publishing France
1, rue st. Georges
75 009 Paris
France

International Thomson Publishing
Southern Africa
Building 19, Constantia Park
239 Old Pretoria Road, P.O. Box 2459
Halfway House, 1685 South Africa

1 2 3 4 5 6 7 8 9 10 QEBFF 01 00 99 98 97 96 95

Library of Congress Cataloging-in-Publication Data (available upon request)

ISBN 1 850-32213 9

CONTENTS

ACKNOWLEDGMENTS

This book is a substantially revised and updated version of a two-volume set originally released by the Software Productivity Consortium. This revision was written by Dr. Richard T. Bechtold, with concept review and contributions provided by Linda Gates. Dr. Bechtold was also the principal author of all prior versions of this material. Additionally, Dr. John Brackett and Dr. Sam Redwine were significant contributors to earlier versions.

The consortium thanks the Vitro Software Engineering Process Group members: Walt Greenspon, Rick Emery, Pauline Martin, Herb Nachmann, and Ed Zarrella, and the Vitro Corporation for their participation in a process definition pilot project. Valuable insights were gained—and numerous improvements made—in the consortium's process definition methodology and techniques as a direct result of their work.

The consortium also thanks Alice Forey and Jennifer McLaughlin, SYSCON SEPG members. Their early use of the revised process templates resulted in significant improvements to the material presented here.

In addition to formal pilot projects, numerous recommendations for how to perform process improvement and process representation have been received from across the consortium's member companies. (At the time of writing, these included Aerojet, Boeing, EER, GDE Systems, Intermetrics, Lockheed-Martin, Northrop-Grumman, PRB Associates, Rockwell, SEMA Inc., Space Applications, and United Technologies.) Their advice and support are gratefully acknowledged and appreciated.

This material is based in part on work sponsored by the Advanced Research Projects Agency under Grant MDA972-92-J-1018. The content does not necessarily reflect the position or the policy of the U.S. government, and no official endorsement should be inferred.

1

INTRODUCTION

1.1 PURPOSE AND SCOPE

The objective of this book is to guide you in performing process improvement by efficiently developing and evolving a quality set of process definitions that will direct and improve the ways you develop software—both to improve your products and process and to allow assessment at the Department of Defense Software Engineering Institute's (SEI) Capability Maturity Model (CMM)[1] Levels 2 (Repeatable) and 3 (Defined). You should be better able to engineer your process descriptions and the processes themselves after reading this book.

1.1.1 A Practical Approach to Process Definition

This book offers a practical approach to reflecting experience and distilled research and includes insights gained from significant, real-world application. This approach has several characteristics that help ensure a successful process definition and modeling effort. For example, the incremental process definition methodology (IPDM):

- Provides how-to guidance for early success and a sound foundation for continuing success.

- Organizes the definition as it is developed.

- Avoids unnecessarily elaborate or formal notations.

- Is driven by your goals.

---

[1] Capability Maturity Model (CMM) has been service marked by Carnegie-Mellon University.

- Considers your context and the factors you need to deal with in your situation.

- Exploits simple automation to generate and revise books and other materials rapidly.

- Directly supports management (including self-management) of the process definition effort.

Organizations need to have a representation option that combines the strengths of text- and graphic-based representations while minimizing their respective weaknesses. IPDM is specifically designed to support process representation as three separate yet tightly integrated concerns: (1) design, development, and implementation of the process model; (2) generation of various output products, such as books and training material, from your process model; and (3) management and review of the development of both the process model and the derived output products.

The data-organizing templates presented in this book can be rendered as paper templates, but their design directly facilitates automated templates via mainstream information management repositories. Examples of template fields are text-oriented descriptions of activities, pre- and postconditions, internal processing, comments, role descriptions, product descriptions, risk types and levels, and revision history. Through a variety of relationships, the templates also convey an explicit architecture directly supporting graphical rendering and analysis. This combined template-based and graphically based approach provides you greater opportunity for the optimal combination of both text and diagrams toward the cost-effective development and use of process representations.

1.1.2 Process Definition Goals

There are numerous goals for process definition:

- To improve your processes organization-wide, such as through a total quality management (TQM) initiative.

- To reduce process management or technical problems.

- To respond to customer or market pressures to improve or certify, such as SEI CMM or ISO 9000.

- To reach aggressive business goals.

- To augment or replace existing process documentation that is either unused or too expensive to maintain.

Process definitions are needed for the same reasons sports teams need playbooks. A team without a playbook must transfer everything from head to head, typically through long apprenticeship; is only as good as what is in their heads, has more trouble adjusting and improving plays; scratches their changes only in the dirt; and can never be on the same page. Though they do different things with them, playbooks are important to both coaches and players; they are an essential organizational asset.

Every organization, regardless of size or maturity, has a process for developing and maintaining its products or rendering services. When using a defined process, your organization may experience some of the following benefits:

- **Improved productivity (and teamwork)** because communication among the process users, managers, process developers, and customers is more effective.

- **Reduced rework** because you identify and eliminate problems early in the process rather than later.

- **Efficient project staff start-up time** because there is a documented process for training.

- **Reduced development costs** due to reduced volatility in software development processes.

- **Improved predictability of budgets and schedules** because you have defined what to measure, when to measure it, and how to use the information.

- **Improved tool usage** because tool usage is defined and supported by training material.

- **Faster project start-up** because the project has a process that it can tailor.

- **Increased integration among resulting products** due to improved coordination among and communication between teams.

- **Increased quality of the resulting products** because reviews are defined and understood to be an integral part of the process.

Existing examples of process representations include policy, procedures, and operational manuals developed by organizations to inform and guide their employees in the performance of their responsibilities. Most organizational process guidebooks only define the process, but a few make use of relatively high-level or simple process models.

Although process modeling is a comparatively rare technique for representing organizational processes, it is a well-known and mature technique for representing systems implemented by computer systems. Example techniques include statecharts, structured analysis and design technique (SADTs), and the entry-task-validation-exit (ETVX) paradigm. Due to fundamental parallels between defining and modeling organizational processes and computer-based systems processes, you can apply many techniques from systems process representation to organizational process representation. Similarly, many of the advantages and benefits derived by building computer process representations can also be derived from organizational process representations.

1.1.3 Goal-Driven Approach

Unfortunately, probably as many attempts at process definition fail as succeed. This is particularly true in any domain involving high technology, especially when software engineering is a significant part of the process. The job is not simple or intuitive and can fail in a number of ways: undertaking the wrong scope; trying to define too much too soon; ignoring existing staff, process, or culture; over- or underdesigning of process; using inappropriate techniques for process definition; developing an inconsistent or rigid definition; producing guidebooks that are not used; updating too slowly; and loss of sponsorship or support due to cost or schedule overruns within the process definition effort. To avoid these types of failures, you need to define specific goals clearly—for example:

- Analyze process (in)efficiencies.

- Identify and remove process redundancies.

- Identify and eliminate areas where the process is unknown or undefined.

- Gain insights into process risk.

- Identify where, when, and how process metrics will be collected and used.

The key point is that it is important to allow your goals to drive your process definition effort. If the goal is to analyze the representation for process bottlenecks, this will influence the type of representation that should be constructed. If the goal is to identify and remove process redundancy, eliminate areas where the process remains largely undefined, seek insights into process risk, or establish or analyze a metrics program, all these considerations influence not only the type of definition or model constructed but also the approach taken in researching and constructing those representations. This issue is examined in detail in Chapter 3.

Process representation can span the effort spectrum from easy to exceedingly difficult as a function of process complexity and desired level of detail:

- Initially, you may find that relatively simple diagrams of isolated parts of the process are sufficient to achieve your immediate goals.

- Later, you may find that you can achieve additional goals by extending your existing representation, adding more detail, and maybe capturing primary interrelationships between your growing inventory of process asset models.

- Still later, other goals may be achieved through even further expansion of scope, detail, abstraction, and information.

The magnitude of your goals must be directly related to the magnitude of organizational support for process representation. This book, and the tools and techniques it proposes, have been designed to facilitate precisely this type of goal-driven, incremental approach to process definition and modeling.

1.2 INTENDED AUDIENCE AND USES

The intended audience for this book includes practitioners interested in developing process definition(s) that are acceptable for SEI Level 2 or 3 assessments, ISO 9000 certification, and those interested in the tangible benefit derived from applying process definition and modeling techniques and methods including automation. This audience is primarily:

- Software engineering process group (SEPG) members.

- Process action teams.

- Process engineers and modelers.

Line engineers, project managers, and anyone else working on or interested in the area of process analysis, design, development, improvement, or management can also benefit from this book. Because most of the intended readers are not necessarily familiar with the issues and aspects of process definition, representation, and modeling, motivation and rationale behind the recommended techniques are provided throughout the book.

This book can help you:

- Establish a common foundation for process engineering, training, and documentation.

- Develop process-oriented guidebooks, improve their usability, or reduce their cost.

- Develop process training and education.

- Improve your process either in general, for ISO 9000 certification, or to CMM Level 2 or 3.

- Construct process representations either generally or based on SADT, ETVX, or another process representation paradigm.

- Model your processes in a manner that facilitates process reverse engineering or process reengineering.

Although this book can be useful in a variety of contexts, it particularly benefits people and organizations who work with or depend on software-intensive high technology and must develop a process improvement action plan calling for definition of parts or all of their processes.

This book introduces both fundamental and advanced process definition concepts, explains how to develop a definition, and provides nontechnical as well as technical advice. Most of the text focuses on examples of software development processes. However, the vast majority of the principles are equally applicable to process improvement within any other complex process or business area. Additionally, although you can use this book by itself, you are also provided with relevant references to other material.

This book provides a flexible set of techniques and data-organizing templates for capturing and representing processes and explains how to use the template-based information to produce process-oriented guidebooks, training materials, and models. The material is presented so that it is usable to achieve basic objectives (such as producing process guidebooks and training material) efficiently and rapidly. This material also shows a migration path by which you can incrementally progress to more advanced applications of process improvement and process engineering that support, for instance, process simulation and automated enactment.

1.3 ORGANIZATION

The structure of the rest of this book is as follows:

- Chapter 2, "Process Definition Basics": Presents the role of process definition within an organization and fundamental process definition concepts; it shows where and how you use process definitions and introduces IPDM.

- Chapter 3, "Incremental Process Representation and Process Improvement": Discusses how to determine your objectives, identify your constraints, and select your process representation tasks. A 15-step sequence of tasks is described to guide you through analyzing, designing, developing, validating, and fielding improved processes. This chapter concludes with an explanation of process models—their types and their usage.

- Chapter 4, "Key Elements of Process Improvement": Examines process improvement from the organizational perspective and examines key issues relating to ensuring the success of organizational process improvement. Primary subjects are change and change management; introducing process definition into your organization; using metrics to steer toward success;

training-oriented process representations; and top-down versus bottom-up process improvement.

- Chapter 5, "Process Templates": Returns to the details of process information collection and management, especially with regard to using commercial tools to facilitate the process improvement program. This chapter describes the conceptual model behind the information-gathering templates and goal-based process definition, and it suggests a variety of types of process information that you may need to collect, describe, or manage as part of your process improvement effort. Discussion is included to help you identify the subset of process information that is critical for you to collect and manage to have a robust and successful approach to process improvement.

- "Abbreviations and Acronyms": Contains abbreviations and acronyms used in this guidebook and their definitions.

- "Glossary": Contains a list of terms used in this guidebook and their definitions.

- "References": Contains sources cited in this guidebook.

- "Bibliography": Contains additional sources of information.

1.4 AUTHOR INTERACTION AND FEEDBACK

The consortium is interested in end-user reaction, case studies, feedback, pilot projects, and any suggestions or recommendations for improving and advancing the content of this book. While insights from researchers and technologists are also appreciated, the consortium is especially interested in feedback from those actively involved in process improvement and producing process definitions. The consortium encourages you to apply the information presented and strongly encourages feedback on how to make this information more useful to you and others. Contact Software Productivity Consortium, SPC Building, 2214 Rock Hill Road, Herndon, Virginia 22070 (703) 742-7211. Ask for (or write to) the process definition technology manager in the Systematic Process Improvement Division.

Chapter
2

PROCESS DEFINITION BASICS

2.1 THE ROLE OF PROCESS DEFINITION

Defining process is crucial to the success of any process improvement effort. This chapter covers the context, concepts, and activities of process definition and prepares you for the remainder of this book. Process definition and modeling activities—jointly referred to as representation—are an integral part of, and therefore conducted in the context of, process improvement and process engineering.

2.1.1 Process Definition as Part of Process Improvement

Defining and modeling your process is typically part of any process improvement effort. Many process improvement plans call for incrementally defining a process as an early step in an improvement program and a requirement to meet assessment or certification goals. Success of process definitions depends on their fit to, and acceptance by, all the affected persons and organizational units, as well as their technical merit. Only by understanding and involving all the stakeholders, combined with process competence, can success be expected. Recognized need to change, management support, a strong influential advocate, adequate resources, and supportive initial users are all important to obtain maximum value from a process definition effort.

Process definitions have many uses, including guiding persons to do successful work and providing an explicit representation of a process that can be analyzed and changed in the pursuit of improvement. Although it may be difficult to achieve, a definition of an improved process is still only a limited part of improving the process. The process of defining a process also affects process improvement.

To be consistently successful, process definition efforts need to be part of a well-planned and -implemented process improvement effort. This is discussed in greater detail in Chapter 4, but for an overview, consider the cyclic process for process improvement involving 15 major activities in five groups shown in Figure 2-1 (Software Productivity Consortium 1993a):

9

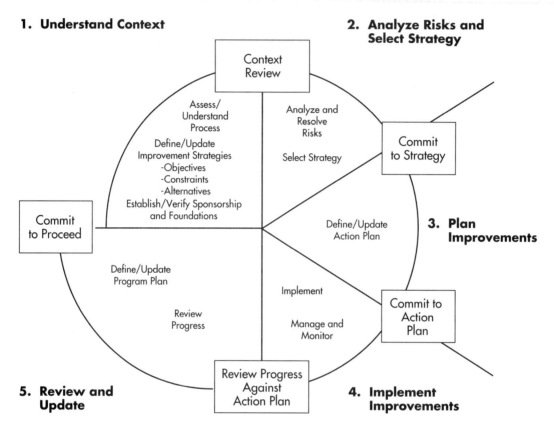

Figure 2-1. *Process Improvement Process*

1. **Understand context.** Understand the current context, including support for improvement, and the current development process. A process assessment is frequently performed as part of understanding the current context.

2. **Analyze risks and select strategy.** Analyze risks in continuing to follow the current process. Select a strategy for incremental implementation of improvements to the existing process.

3. **Plan improvements.** Create a prioritized action plan for improvement, and commit the resources required to implement the action plan.

4. **Implement improvements.** Implement the process improvements according to the action plan, and monitor projects in order to monitor the impact of the process improvements.

5. **Review and update.** Review progress and decide how to proceed with the next process improvement iteration.

Multiple improvement iterations are required since process change must be gradual and continuous. Because the culture within an organization must change, evolution from current practice is preferable to massive process changes.

Many of the process definition and modeling activities described in this book fit into the Understand Context and Implement Improvements activities shown in Figure 2-1. In the Understand Context activity, the present process must be understood to provide the foundations for process improvement decisions. In the Implement Improvements activity, an improved process will be defined as part of carrying out an action plan.

2.1.2 Process Definition as Part of Process Engineering

Software is developed and evolved using a system involving complex processes. Experience has shown that for consistently good results, such complex processes need to be engineered using organizationally sensitive approaches, knowledge of the domain and relevant technology, openness to change, and a thorough understanding of users and requirements. Process engineering and process definition are closely related and are best thought of as two ends of the continuum of process improvement. Process engineering tends to address higher-level aspects of process improvement, such as organizational change management. Process definition and modeling are more involved with how-to issues. Consequently, although this book contains a considerable amount of material on process engineering, the primary focus remains practical. In other words, although some theory is provided, the application of that theory is considered of paramount importance and will be stressed.

This book is, in part, a contribution to the relatively young field of process engineering (and especially, software process engineering), but much of the advice provided is similar to what one would also find in successful systems and industrial engineering. Therefore, you should build on what you already know about how to do systems analysis, design, verification and validation, and the introduction of improved technology in similar organizational settings. Examples you can learn from include the following:

- The process of discovering what is really happening in an organization.

- The advantages of iterative over big-bang approaches.

- The importance of risk management.

- The need to provide for variations for use in different situations.

- The centrality of people and organizational issues to success.

To understand better how to pursue process improvement via low-cost, high-value process definition and modeling activities you need to understand a number of basic concepts related to process representation.

2.2 CONCEPTS

Process representations—definitions and models—exist at different levels of generality within different levels of an organization, can be expressed using a variety of notations, styles, and formats, and are developed for different purposes.

2.2.1 Levels of Process Definition

As shown in Figure 2-2, process definitions can exist at several levels, including organizational, business area, program, and project levels. (This subject is revisited in detail in Chapter 5. Only basic principles are presented here.) Process improvement activities can start at any level. In many cases process definitions are first prepared for a subset of the activities performed on a project. For example, a detailed definition of an improved configuration management process might be developed on a project and then generalized at the program level to be applicable to projects of different sizes. Alternatively, the configuration management process might be defined at the program level and provided to projects with guidance on how to specialize or tailor it based on project size and implementation environment.

Over time, an organization will build up "process assets," which assist projects in creating a project-specific process. Using the terminology of the SEI, these assets can be divided into three groups:

1. **Software process kernels.** Kernels specify fundamental activities that are likely to be performed on many projects (i.e., configuration management).

2. **Software life-cycle models.** These models define the sequence of activities performed during the software life cycles appropriate for an organization's software products. For example, one project may elect to use the "waterfall" model, while another may decide to implement an incremental development life-cycle model.

3. **Process architectures.** At one or more levels, process architectures show major process steps or relationships, how those steps or relationships interact, and how process kernels fit within the architecture.

The guidance and techniques presented in this book apply to all three types of assets.

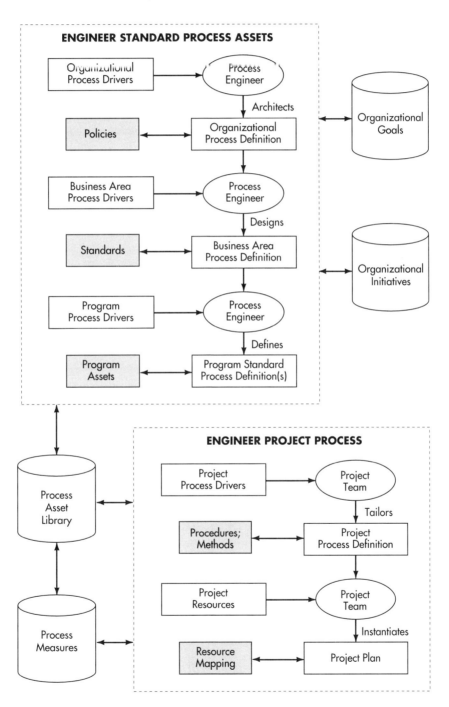

Figure 2-2*. Abstraction Levels for Process Definitions*

2.2.2 Contents of Process Definitions

Any process definition must describe what the process does, who does it, what products and resources are needed, and what products are produced. Detailed process definitions should contain sufficient information for the process to be carried out successfully (i.e., enacted) as defined. The definition will usually require, or assume the existence of, a certain level of personnel skills and appropriate resources. Skills and resources essential for successful enactment need to be described in the process definition. (Chapters 3 and 5 describe the contents of process definitions in detail.)

At a minimum, this book describes a process in terms of three useful abstractions:

1. Activities that are performed.

2. Products to indicate the things used and produced. (Products produced as a result of process definition and modeling are referred to as end products.)

3. Roles to describe who performs the activity.

A process representation will describe many relationships among these three types of abstractions—for example:

- One activity verifies the work of another activity.

- A role performs an activity.

- A product is produced by an activity.

Processes are dynamic in nature, and so describing process behavior over time is a critical part of developing a process definition. You need to include the following types of process behavioral information in your process definition:

- Under what circumstances can an activity begin?

- What must happen for a product to be considered approved?

- What are the entry and exit criteria for an activity?

- Where can you choose from a set of alternative activities?

An activity description describes both what is to be done and how it is to be accomplished. The steps for accomplishing the activity can be represented in many ways, ranging from a textual description to a detailed algorithmic specification. Alternative descriptions of how may be provided; for example, the activity "requirements definition" could be carried out for a particular application by using an object-oriented analysis method. In many cases, a process definition will reference separately documented procedures or methods.

2.2.3 Process Definition End-Product Formality

A process definition document (or a process guidebook) is written for the people who will enact the process. Process definitions can also be written for execution by computers and are frequently called *process programs.* However, the primary subject of this guidebook is how to prepare process definitions that can be effectively used by people.

The staff defining the process (process engineers) must gather a large amount of information and organize it in order to produce understandable guidebooks, usable training material, and so forth. Various modeling techniques have been developed that help process engineers with the information-gathering and organizational tasks. For a modeling technique to be useful to process engineers, it must describe:

- The relevant abstractions: activities, products, and roles.

- The required relationships among these three abstractions of the process.

- The behavior of the activities, products, and roles over time.

Process definition end products can be characterized by their degree of formality:

- Unconstrained descriptive text

- Template-based descriptions

- Constrained graphical models

- Executable graphical models or process grammars

- Mathematical notations

The most common technique for representing processes is the use of text. However, the potential for inconsistency, ambiguity, and uncertainty is considerable. Therefore, an increasing number of process engineers are using more precisely defined notations to support their work in understanding and analyzing processes.

Having graphical support for a notation can directly contribute to having some degree of formality. Usually a graphically oriented notation comes coupled with a method that imposes rules on placement, use, and connections among the graphical objects. These rules constrain the types of structures that can be built and increase the formality of the resulting depictions. Additionally, graphical depictions are especially useful for portraying abstract or high-level relationships. Historically, the graphical techniques used most frequently by process engineers are integrated definition (IDEF), SADT, and structured analysis. The techniques described in this guidebook are compatible with and supportive of generating diagrams consistent with these and other techniques. However, if you want to avoid the complexities involved in generating such formalized pictures, there is a less formal graphical notation presented in Chapter 3. Finally, extremely formal descriptions involve extensive use of mathematical notations.

An important capability of a modeling method is the ability to represent how processes can be broken down, or decomposed, into subprocesses. Process decomposition usually is done by decomposing the activities and identifying the relevant products and required resources with each subactivity. One of the principal reasons for using a graphical modeling method is to show several levels of decomposition and the relationships of the subprocesses (i.e., how the output of one activity is used as an input to another activity).

Most modeling techniques use formal or semiformal notations that are too obscure or complex for practitioners to accept in guidebooks or training material. A guidebook should describe what its intended reader needs to know and should be written so that readers can easily access needed information. Therefore, the preparation of a usable guidebook involves much more work than just repackaging a process definition model prepared by a process engineer. Chapters 3 through 5 provide suggestions on developing and maintaining usable guidebooks, training material, and other process-intensive material.

2.2.4 Goal-Driven Process Representation

Process representation spans the entire spectrum, from very easy to exceedingly difficult, as a function of process complexity, intended usage, and desired level of detail. Before an organization undertakes process definition and modeling, it needs to define the audience for the process definition results and the specific objectives that it expects. If the goal is process reengineering to improve productivity and reduce process redundancy, the type of definition or model constructed by process engineers is likely to be significantly different than if the goal is to produce training materials for a process that remains largely undefined. Accordingly, the approach taken in researching and constructing these representations will vary.

The magnitude of goals should be directly related to the magnitude of organizational support for process representation. If the organization can support a process representation effort only nominally, the goals must be kept realistically small. Conversely, if an organization is prepared to give considerable support, then the goals can be correspondingly larger.

The key point is that it is important to allow goals to drive the process representation effort. Initially, relatively simple diagrams of parts of the process are sufficient to achieve immediate goals. Later, you may find that you can achieve additional goals by extending your existing process representations, adding more detail, and perhaps packaging the representation as a process kernel that can be tailored for use on multiple projects.

Understanding the audience for the work will help define goals. A process definition for use by staff with experience in performing the process can focus on providing detail in high-risk areas while providing minimum constraints in areas where good professional judgment is an adequate guide. If your goal is to produce a process guidebook and training materials for new, junior employees, more detail in most process steps will be required. The

IPDM presented in this guidebook has been designed to facilitate this type of goal-driven, incremental approach to process definition and representation.

2.3 OVERVIEW OF PROCESS DEFINITION ACTIVITIES

IPDM is applicable across a wide spectrum of organizations with different process engineering needs. In a typical organization, some organizational standards based on a widely used life-cycle model may exist, but the standards may only specify milestones to be completed and the characteristics of products to be produced. Since few reusable, enactable software process kernels exist in most organizations, a potential starting point for process definition work is creating process kernels needed for one project that are likely to be useful to other projects. Examples of areas for creating such kernels are configuration management, testing, project planning, peer reviews, and quality assurance.

Unfortunately, the typical maturity of the process definition process itself is initially low. This guidebook emphasizes elements that help you start effectively and improve with experience. If you are aiming toward having a defined software process, the process definition effort should define its process too. Chapter 3 describes the 15 steps associated with IPDM in detail. For now, however, we can consider process definition to consist generally of following five activities:

- Process end-product specification

- Process definition planning

- Process familiarization

- Iterative process definition development

- End-product generation

2.3.1 Process End-Product Specification

The objective of this activity is a clear specification of the end product(s) that will result from the process definition and modeling effort, the goals of these specific end products, their audience, scope, level of detail, and so on. Achieving a clear, shared explicit statement of the goals that reflect the user's needs for the process end product is a key to success. Setting goals that are compatible with the resources available to the process engineers is also important and must be the basis for all process definition planning. One strategy is to generate initially the process definition end product at the project level, test it with project staff, and then develop a tailorable version for use throughout an organization. Producing the organizational version will typically involve removing project-specific detail and focusing on the constraints that must guide any implementation of the process. As a consequence, process definitions at the organizational level should be sparse, "low-side-compliant" process descriptions that preserve, and pass through to the project level, the greatest amount of freedom possible.

If, for example, the process end products will be a configuration management guidebook and a training course, important issues to process engineers deciding on the goals for these products would be the following:

- Whether the products are intended for both small and large projects.

- Whether the audience is the entire development staff or only configuration management specialists.

- What type of automated support will be assumed.

Some typical questions you might ask about the audience are:

- Who will use the process definition end product?

- What do they need to know to fulfill their current responsibilities?

- What vocabulary do they use?

- What experience do they have in performing the current process?

- How much effort are they willing to put into understanding the process definition end product?

If the planned audience cannot enact the process efficiently and correctly, the effort will fail. One of the goals of IPDM is to facilitate end product verification by rapid, iterative generation of process definition end products. This is achieved through automated support using low-cost, commercially available tools (e.g., database, word processing, and graphics packages). Since producing the perfect guidebook the first time is impossible, your goal should be to create increasingly effective versions as you obtain (pilot) project feedback.

2.3.2 Process Definition Planning

The objective of this activity is to verify that the scope of work is consistent with the resources available, and the necessary products can be produced within the necessary time and budget constraints.

Establishing the scope of the process definition effort needs careful consideration, particularly at the beginning. Among the factors to consider are the objectives for the product, resources available, time period available for the effort, cost and benefits, and cooperation expected from information sources outside the process definition team. You need to verify your initial statement of scope against process improvement plans and validate it with all affected parties. Although overall management support may exist for the process improvement effort, you should also seek sponsorship from the management of the portion of the organization that must assist the process definition team and who will use the process definition end product.

The process definition effort should be treated as a miniproject, with a project plan, measurable milestones, a schedule, and resource requirements. Agreement is needed on how to validate the completeness, correctness, and usability of the process definition products. You will select the method and notation to be used by process engineers. You will also decide how the process definition end products will be produced by the process engineers.

2.3.3 Process Familiarization

The objective of this activity is to obtain as much context as possible for the process definition work. This activity consists of three major subactivities:

1. Review existing process documentation.

2. Identify roles of key personnel in the process.

3. Develop process context diagram.

With minimum impact on current operations, you can gather a great deal of information about the current process and the local terminology from existing process documentation, even if the existing documents are underutilized. Other useful sources are corporate standards, contractually binding regulations, organizational charts, and position descriptions. Your goal is to locate the most relevant materials, review them, and gain an understanding of the key activities and products involved in the process. You also want to identify the roles of key personnel and organizations in performing the process.

Some useful questions to ask to become familiar with the process are:

- What are the primary products and services provided by the process?

- What organizations are the consumers of these products and services?

- What organizations provide products, services, and resources needed to perform the process?

- What are all the organizational elements involved in performing the process?

The answers to these questions will help you to assess the value of the information you have collected and to make a plan for gathering missing information. Interviews are helpful for gathering additional information, whether you are documenting an existing process or defining an improved process for future adoption. Interviews will probably identify many hidden requirements and constraints that must be satisfied for a process to be readily accepted.

Also valuable is the use of review teams to carry out a review process that will build consensus regarding the actual or desired process. The ideal team should include process practitioners and senior technical and managerial staff with in-depth knowledge of the process. There are fields within the process templates specifically intended to facilitate this review process.

A useful way to organize the information you have been gathering is to create a diagram that describes the current flow of products between the process being defined and the external consumers and producers. Once you have confirmed these external interfaces to the process, make a list of three to ten major activities and the most important products involved in the current process. Later you may redefine these activities and products, but this initial overview of the process will help you organize the materials you need to gather.

2.3.4 Iterative Process Definition Development

The objective of this activity is to develop your process definition rapidly while maintaining a high level of end-user involvement and feedback. This activity consists of three major subactivities:

1. Data gathering and analysis of results.

2. Model construction.

3. Verification and review.

The key to successful data gathering is to find out what is really going on, not what is supposed to be going on. If you need to conduct interviews, a useful way of obtaining maximum value from the interview is to have the subject describe the steps of producing a product that is an external output of the process and to describe their role in performing the process activities. Ask the interviewee to think in terms what has to be accomplished before the activity can take place, what the process inputs and outputs are, and what the criteria are for completion of the activity.

In the second subactivity, model construction, process engineers prepare a representation of the process to understand and analyze the process and to communicate with the review team. IPDM, including the template-based process description described in Chapter 3, is one possible representation approach.

The result of the model construction subactivity is not the process definition end product. Whatever the form of model used, the last step in the process definition process will be to produce the process definition end product to be used by process practitioners. Whatever approach you select, you must carefully consider how that approach supports end product generation. Having elaborate IDEF diagrams is of questionable value if only 1% of your audience can—or is willing to take the time to—interpret those diagrams correctly.

Building a model helps the process engineer examine the relationships within the information gathered and identify errors, missing data, or inconsistent data. The evolving model will document the current state of the process engineer's understanding of the process and will focus attention on where more information gathering is required. The process of building models is described in Chapter 3.

The objective of the verification and review subactivity is to determine whether the process definition work faithfully represents the process being described and whether the model is a satisfactory basis for producing the process definition end products. A recommended part of the verification process is a walk-through of the model by the process engineers to show the reviewers what the model is intended to communicate.

2.3.5 End-Product Generation

Multiple end products may need to be produced from the process representation; examples are guidebooks for new project members, checklists for use by experienced practitioners, and training materials for new employees.

Producing process end products, once their goals have been defined, is largely an information management problem, not a word processing problem. Word processors principally help only in the presentation of information, not in the management of that information. Maintaining relationships among your process information and extracting subsets of that information requires the representation to be stored in a highly structured form.

Another aspect of the information management problem is how to produce updated process definition end products quickly and efficiently. The goal is to avoid one of the prime reasons for unused documentation: everyone knowing that the actual practice evolved out from under the documented approach. The approach presented in this book is completely compatible with the use of simple database management systems to support producing multiple products from the process representation and for easily regenerating them as the process representation is better understood, refined, and updated.

2.4 PROCESS DEFINITION NEEDS

Process definition can satisfy a variety of needs. Your organizational process improvement goals will substantially affect how you conduct your process definition and modeling effort. Most organizational process improvement goals can be mapped to the following five needs:

1. To perform successful work.

2. To facilitate training.

3. To improve the process being used.

4. To engineer new processes.

5. To automate processes.

This guidebook addresses all five needs.

2.4.1 Perform Successful Work

An organization needs the ability to perform successful work repetitively and consistently. This ability is not only necessary for one division or group, but it may also be important for multiple divisions or groups to perform the same type of work in the same way simultaneously. Having a defined process directly supports having a repeatable process. Although work may be successfully repeated in the absence of a defined process, such repetition depends entirely on the efforts of individuals. Conversely, once a process is defined, it can become institutionalized and preserved by the organization.

2.4.2 Facilitate Training

Another key use of process representations is to facilitate training. Training employees in their respective processes improves the likelihood that they understand the key characteristics of the process they should be following, which can quickly lead to higher employee productivity, efficiency, and morale. Note that it is not the process representation itself that yields these benefits but the training opportunities that result from having a representation of the process.

2.4.3 Improve the Process

As the Department of Defense (1988) total quality management plan said, "The first step is to identify and define the processes by which work is accomplished." Engineering of processes is usually part of improvement.

2.4.3.1 Preserve Lessons

Key advantages to representing a process are the preservation of lessons learned and insights gained from performing that process. Typically, processes evolve. People involved in either managing or participating within the process often find a variety of ways to improve how they perform their work. Unless a process is defined, there is an increased risk that as individuals move to work in other areas, their process improvement insights move with them. By having a representation of a process and by updating that representation to reflect process improvements, the insights and lessons learned through performing a process are preserved.

2.4.3.2 Transfer Process

The existence of a process definition helps both to propagate a process within an organization or project and to transfer better processes in from outside. Transfer success is aided if the definition includes introductory, training, and reference material suitable for all the roles involved in transfer, use, and evolution.

2.4.4 Engineer New Processes

Engineering of a process is applicable across any phase of a process life span: its creation, improvement, and replacement. This book emphasizes the definition, modeling, analysis, and similar design and implementation aspects of process engineering.

2.4.4.1 Define

Definition methods and representations are central to the activity of defining processes. The material in this book supports both creating a new process (for defining either a new process or the next generation of an existing process) and defining a process already in existence.

2.4.4.2 Analyze and Compare

One of the most important key uses of process representation is to facilitate the analysis and comparison of both existing and proposed processes. In the absence of process representations, detailed analysis of existing or proposed processes is difficult, if not impossible. All discussion on the process would be based on individual experience and opinion. Typically, there needs to be a consensus on what the process is before the focus can be turned to how the process can be improved. Without a process representation, valuable time and energy are lost while analysts attempt to reach agreement on their differing impressions of the process. By defining and creating a variety of simple models of a process, the key characteristics of the process are communicated more consistently and less ambiguously. This tends to minimize confusion about what the process is and frees process analysts to focus on how to analyze and improve that process.

2.4.5 Automate Processes

Two motivations for automated or executable process definitions are automated support and simulation. While this guidebook gives them limited treatment, you should be aware these are two areas with strong future potential. Automated processes can directly contribute to process analysis, planning, improvement, and training.

2.4.5.1 Automated Support

Over the last decade, a series of international software process workshops has been held, mainly inspired by the potential for automated support. Although they are limited, early products are beginning to appear. These products are not only targeted to software process support but to office work flow and business reengineering. Some groupware products have potential for process support. Scripts or more advanced mechanisms are steadily advancing. These mechanisms can compose and orchestrate the execution of multiple tools, when needed, with little or no human action.

Although automated support is an area with more promise than actual products, it is still important to both mid- and long-term planning.

2.4.5.2 Simulation

Simulation tools originally intended for other or general-purpose uses have been used to try to simulate software processes. Software process simulation experience is very limited but shows some promise for engineering, management, and training. The creation of "virtual projects" with stochastic simulation allows both analysis of what may happen and case studies for training. One advantage is that the effects of the stochastic and multiple-feedback-loop nature of projects and organizations are much easier to appreciate with some of these simulation techniques.

As in all other modeling of human organizations, many questions exist about the appropriate purpose, scope, and fidelity for a model to be useful. Definitions that can be modeled and instantiated to degrees needed for useful simulation will offer significant advantages in the long term. Chapter 5 offers process information extensions that support the improvement of definitions over time toward increasingly rigorous and formal descriptions suitable for simulation and other automated analysis. Recent dramatic improvements in the user interface of process simulation and enactment tools, coupled with significant price reductions, now make process simulation an increasingly important part of process improvement.

2.5 DOCUMENTING YOUR PROCESS USING IPDM

IPDM includes a flexible set of templates, optional graphic notation, and various techniques for capturing and representing processes and for representing the relationships and constraints between and within the products, roles, and activities comprising the processes. IPDM provides guidance on the content of process and method descriptions and their use. In addition to presenting IPDM fundamentals, examples are provided throughout the text.

In general, IPDM is an information-centered methodology, combined with a goal-driven process representation strategy, so that the definitions will meet your constraints and needs. To collect and organize information, various classes of process templates are used (e.g., activity, product, and support templates). Automated support for producing guidebooks and training material from this template-based definition is readily achievable through a variety of commercially available integrated tool suites. Even a relatively simple database implementation can substantially improve your efficiency and effectiveness in collecting, managing, repackaging and distributing process information.

Figure 2-3 describes how your process definition is used to generate different types of end products. You use templates to gather process information and organize and verify it both for consistency and completeness. You use an accompanying graphic representation that maps from the templates and allows a better overall view of the process definition.

IPDM has evolved with lessons learned from several real-world application projects and contains a number of characteristics that help make it practical. It explicitly identifies and organizes the kinds of information needed and is understandable by both management and engineers. It supports incremental improvement in both process definitions and in the

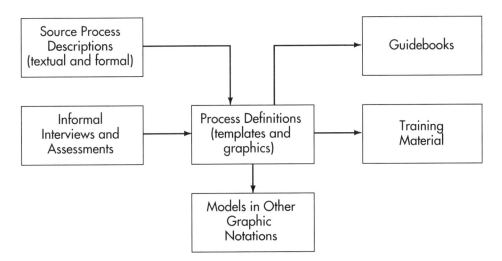

Figure 2-3. Kinds of Process Descriptions

process of process definition. It does not require esoteric notations or skills yet can be used to define complex processes. Thus, IPDM is suitable for organizations just beginning process improvement and for organizations with advanced process experience and correspondingly advanced requirements.

3

INCREMENTAL PROCESS REPRESENTATION AND PROCESS IMPROVEMENT

The core phases of process improvement are process analysis, design, development, and delivery. Each phase critically depends on varying forms of process representations. Process representations, which include both definitions and models, are abstractions of the process. You can use these abstractions to answer many different types of questions about the process. Various types of models answer different questions effectively, and no single process representation can answer all the key questions about the process. The type of representation to be developed invariably depends on the audience.

The objective of a process representation, or model, is to emphasize important characteristics and reduce or eliminate nonessential information based on the needs, background, and orientation of the target audience. The principal intended users of IPDM are process engineers who are performing process improvement activities such as process analysis, process reengineering, process simulation, and the various activities that accompany process improvement, such as producing process guidebooks and training materials for use by people in their organization or project. The material in this chapter specifically targets process engineers.

The first step in successful process representation is to determine your objectives. The second step is to identify the circumstances within which you must work. Section 3.1 assists you in identifying the objectives, circumstances, and tasks that need to be performed. Section 3.2 describes the sequence of steps to follow as you perform the necessary tasks of analyzing, modeling, and defining processes. Section 3.3 describes several types of useful process models and how you can leverage them as you pursue process improvement.

3.1   IDENTIFYING AND SELECTING PROCESS REPRESENTATION TASKS

Before you can select the necessary tasks to perform in process representation, you must first determine your objectives and examine any constraints on the achievement of those objectives. When you have identified objectives and constraints, you can select the tasks you need to perform.

3.1.1   Determining Objectives

Generally, as a process engineer participating in organizational process improvement, your objectives for performing process representation commonly include one or more of the following:

- To disseminate and train the process.

- To analyze and improve the process.

- To plan and control the process.

These are three—not six—distinct objectives. Each of these pairs is, for all practical purposes, inseparable. To disseminate process material, such as guidebooks and procedures, and not provide training is of little, if any, value. Having someone read about the process does not ensure he or she knows how to perform it. Similarly, to attempt to train people in a process that has not been documented or distributed is of little value. Without process documentation, knowledge and techniques acquired during training are easily forgotten.

Analysis and improvement are another single objective. What is the value of analyzing a process if there is no intention of improving it? Similarly, how can you reliably improve a process if you have not first assessed it in terms of relative strengths and weaknesses? The same is true for the objective of planning and controlling the process: it is useless to make plans for something you have no intention of managing, and near impossible to manage something successfully in the absence of plans.

It is critical that you deliberately select what objective(s) you are trying to achieve so that you may focus your efforts on performing only the work that truly needs to be done. Process representation occurs in many forms, and it is quite common for people to waste vast amounts of time and resources building representations that eventually provide little or no contribution toward their actual objectives. In addition to having a clearly defined set of objectives, it is equally important that you perform your work in a manner consistent with your organizational circumstances.

3.1.2 Identifying Circumstances

As shown in Figure 3-1, organizational circumstances can be ranked along a spectrum that ranges from having to be completely reactive to the organization's current situation to being quite proactive. At the reactive end of the scale, your process improvement efforts must have very fast results, even at the expense of long-term value and efficiency. At the proactive end of the scale, you can afford to take an approach that initially requires additional effort, but in time allows for more cost-effective achievement of process improvement objectives.

The most severe type of reactive circumstances is "crisis." Typically, a crisis demands that process improvement work must give the highest priority to reacting to the immediate situation and that no effort should be spent on anything not directly beneficial with regard to resolving the current crisis. Generally, this means getting something—almost anything—on paper fast, and getting it distributed.

The "threat" level of organizational circumstances indicates that a crisis appears imminent. In these circumstances you can exceed doing the bare minimum necessary, but only if there are clear and near-immediate advantages in doing so. This allows you to field a more robust set of process improvement material and support, but usually only if that material is already available and largely reusable. This level of organizational circumstances generally indicates sufficient time to repackage existing material but a lack of time to engage in developing something new.

The "risk" level indicates that you can begin to pursue your process improvement objectives in a manner that offers strategic advantages in addition to the immediate and short-term focus demanded by crisis or threat circumstances, respectively. At this level, you have time for limited new development, but mostly only at a high level. Due to time constraints, most details need to be deferred.

In the absence of needing to respond to immediate or imminent organizational pressures, you should strive to approach process improvement in a manner that helps ensure the maximum organizational benefit over time. At the "prepare" level, your situation allows you to perform value-added work that better positions the organization for the next crisis because

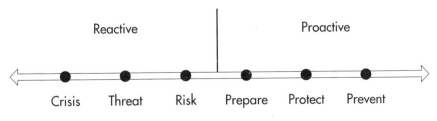

Figure 3-1. *Organizational Circumstances*

circumstances at the moment are relatively calm. These circumstances allow for more time to be spent at process analysis and redesign, versus process capture and documentation.

At the "protect" level, your process improvement work is explicitly intended to yield processes that are sufficiently robust that they can withstand a variety of adverse impacts from circumstances outside the process (or outside of your ability to control). This is achieved through attention to detail, close examination of process dynamics, and effort on ancillary process material such as examples of how processes can be tailored to project-specific characteristics.

Finally, the "prevent" level indicates sufficient time, resources, and support for you to pursue the maximum degree of proactive process improvement. High-fidelity process models, both static and dynamic, allow you to gain detailed insights into the impact of alternative, and sometimes radical, process redesigns. Evaluating, modeling, understanding, and accurately predicting the impact that new, high-technology tools and environments will have on your process is critical at this level. The objective is no longer to prepare for a crisis or even to protect your organization in the event of one. Instead, the objective is to prevent crises from occurring.

Having identified your process improvement objectives and your organizational circumstances, you can explicitly identify and select the process representation tasks that need to be performed.

3.1.3 Selecting Process Representation Tasks

The conceptual framework for process representation reflects three separate tracks, each of which pursues an objective (or more accurately, an inseparable pair of objectives). As shown in Table 3-1, each track is composed of six tiers. Lower tiers in any track are typically all you can do when organizational circumstances mandate a highly reactive approach. Conversely, when organizational circumstances allow you to take a proactive approach, higher tiers of work become increasingly justifiable.

Within each track in the framework, different types of process representations need to be done. The representations tend to be consistent within tracks and different between tracks. For example, process representations intended to disseminate and train the process are generally in the form of process heuristics (rules people need to follow) and are normally quite text intensive. Conversely, representations intended to analyze and improve the process are generally in the form of process models and are quite graphic intensive. Finally, representations intended to plan and control the process occur primarily in the form of logistical representations combined with process measures and metrics and, accordingly, are usually quite numerically intensive. Although there are exceptions to these general characteristics (e.g., process simulation models that are driven by formal, heuristically intensive process programming languages; graphically intensive training material), it is nonetheless important to realize that achieving different objectives *all but mandates* that you take different approaches.

Table 3-1 shows six tiers of process representations for each of the three tracks. Each tier, from top to bottom, represents the need for progressively greater detail, formality, or both, in the process representation. (Increased detail and formality nearly always result in additional time and effort needed to accomplish the work.) Generally, higher tiers build on the work already performed in lower tiers. When lower tiers are skipped and, for example, procedures and methods are written in the absence of policies and standards, there is considerable risk that the resulting work products will be wrong or otherwise unusable. Higher tiers build progressively on the results of lower tiers.

Tier	Track A Disseminate and Train (Text Models)	Track B Analyze and Improve (Graphic Models)	Track C Plan and Control (Numeric Models)
1	Policies	Communication	Plans
2	Standards	Architecture	Schedules
3	Procedures	Interface	Cost
4	Methods	Flow	Status
5	Guidelines	State	Coordination
6	Instances	Simulation	Enactment

Table 3-1. Process Asset Representation Framework

The first track (Track A) includes representations for which the objective is to disseminate and train the process. Each of the six tasks within this track produces process representations that are generally text intensive. The six tiers of Track A are:

1. **Policies.** The objective of this task is to define corporate requirements. Policy statements are typically represented as a set of heuristics that explicitly state what must and must not occur within the organization. Policies are intended, for example, to ensure business objectives and provide for a safe work environment. Policies serve as an internal set of requirements on organizational procedures.

2. **Standards.** This task involves identifying external or widely accepted standards for use within an organization. Commonly, there is a need to tailor these standards so that they fit the organization. On occasion, a set of standards is developed entirely internally (i.e., nothing usable is available from government, industry, academia, or other standards-producing entities). Many standards are

composed of terse statements of process- or product-oriented rules that facilitate ensuring that quality objectives are met.

3. **Procedures.** This task involves defining and providing detailed explanations of what has to happen in order to accomplish the objectives of an activity. Commonly procedures are described in the form of what the activity accomplishes, what inputs are needed, what outputs are generated, who performs the work, what resources are required, how progress of the work is measured, managed, and controlled, and how process and product quality are verified and validated. Often procedures must be made tailorable and are commonly different between different business areas.

4. **Methods.** This task involves writing detailed explanations that provide formulaic instructions on how to perform work. As with cookbooks, well-written methodologies help ensure that a given set of inputs put through a given process following an explicit sequence of steps will reliably produce a particular output—independent of who actually performs the work (presuming, of course, similar levels of competence).

5. **Guidelines.** This task involves augmenting policies, standards, procedures, and methodologies by providing additional heuristics on areas not already covered or only partially covered. Often guidelines consist of information on how to tailor the process information to the specific needs and circumstances of individual projects or programs.

6. **Instances.** This task consists of constructing comprehensive and representative examples of instantiations of processes that are policy and standard compliant and are composed of sets of procedures that are supported by methodologies and guidelines.

The second track (Track B) of the process asset representation framework includes representations to analyze and improve the process:

1. **Architectural.** This task involves building architectural models indicating hierarchical decomposition of both whole-part and generalization-specialization relationships of process objectives (such as activity decomposition into subactivities or product decomposition into subproducts). Architectural models are an important part of communicating organizational procedures.

2. **Interface.** This task consists of building models that explicitly show the assumptions that activities make on the external world: what products are needed as inputs, what products will be produced as outputs, and who is needed to perform the work, for example.

3. **Communication.** Organizations often confuse architectural models of their staff with staff communication models (leading to organization charts with numerous dashed lines, causing no small amount of confusion). Communication models have one purpose: to show who needs to talk to whom within an organization. Detailed communication models may also convey different types of communication, such as commands, status, information, or metrics.

4. **Flow.** The purpose of this task is to build models that show how products, or information, flow from one activity to another. At a minimum, these models strive to ensure that all required inputs to an activity are available from someone and that all generated outputs produced by an activity are used somewhere.

5. **State.** This task consists of building formal models that are executable in computer simulations and strive to ensure consistency and completeness of the temporal implications and characteristics of a process. In particular, state models can be used as a means for assessing the risk or probability of process deadlocks (e.g., everything stops because A is waiting for B, B is waiting for C, and C is waiting for A) and process live-locks (e.g., a subset of the process inadvertently becomes permanently disabled).

6. **Simulation.** The objective of this task is to construct executable models that not only examine the state-transition implications of a given process but also strive to characterize the impact that alternative processes have on cost, schedule, resource utilization, material consumption, and other factors.

The final track (Track C) of the process asset representation framework includes representations whose primary purpose is to support planning and controlling the process. Although many of these representations may appear to be quite text intensive or graphic intensive, this set of representations typically depends extensively on the accuracy and validity of a numeric-intensive foundation. The six tiers of this track are:

1. **Planning.** The purpose of this tier is to build a representation of the process that indicates who does what, to what, using what.

2. **Scheduling.** Once planning is done, the next task is to add the time dimension: when activities are scheduled to occur (predicted start and end dates, resource mappings of who will be doing what, when, etc.).

3. **Costing.** Understanding the cost implications involves building representations that estimate the impact of the plan and schedule on all nontemporal consumables (at a minimum, this includes monetary impact, such as estimated cost to complete, but may also include material impact, especially with regard to finite consumables, or even intangible impacts such as "cost" risk exposure or customer satisfaction).

4. **Status.** As organizations increasingly rely on automated environments to help with and participate in the monitoring and control of processes, one of the first tasks is to build representations (or have the environment generate models) that communicate current status information. This can be of many types (activity status, product development status, resources utilization status, etc.).

5. **Coordination.** Automated process enactment can help ensure that the right (or approved) process is the one being followed. To do so, it is necessary to build models that represent how work coordination will occur, when inspections or reviews are required, when products can or must be submitted into configuration management, and so forth. Typically, these representations help ensure that products do not advance, or work occur, unless certain criteria are met.

6. **Enactment.** This task involves constructing representations that actively participate in process optimization through real-time work environment automated self-monitoring and self-adjustments, and automatic adjustments to plans, schedules, and/or cost representations as a function of feedback from status and coordination representations.

The process asset conceptual framework is useful for ensuring that the right process representations are developed, and they are developed in the right order, for the right reasons. Start at tier 1 and work toward tier 6 iteratively, and only on an as-needed basis. Many organizations mistakenly attempt to build process state or simulation models when they do not yet even understand their basic process architectures.

As a very general guideline, you will find that if your organizational circumstances are crisis or threat, you will likely be focusing on the first couple of tiers; if your circumstances are risk or prepare, then you may be able to afford the time and effort required at tiers 3 and 4; and if your circumstances are protect or prevent, then you should explore the advantages and opportunities conveyed by the extra effort involved in tiers 5 and 6. It is not necessary to pursue each track to exactly the same tier. For example, it may be appropriate for you to pursue Track A to tier 4 (methodologies), Track B to tier 1 (architectural models), and Track C to tier 2 (schedules).

There is no fixed formula. There is only what makes sense for each organization, given its goals and constraints. However, if you find yourself planning to perform tasks at opposite extremes of this framework (such as a pair of tier 1 tracks combined with a tier 6 track), you should realize you're taking a highly unusual approach and should therefore reconfirm whether your approach makes the most sense for your organization.

3.2 THE STEPS OF PROCESS REPRESENTATION

This section describes the IPDM steps for performing efficient, robust, and reliable process representation. This is a recommended approach but by no means the only one. It can serve as a good point of departure for an organization that does not have a history of, or strong preference for, using a different technique.

The scenario uses a top-down approach to process definition based on decomposing the process into activities and tasks, and products to increasing levels of detail. The decomposition process is similar to that recommended in other process modeling techniques such as IDEF and SADT. If a large number of reusable process assets (such as existing representations) exist in an organization, a scenario based on process composition beginning with the process assets could be preferable. Another approach would be to start with the products that are the output of the process and identify activities that create or transform intermediate products to produce the process outputs. Generally you will find the scenario provided below to be a practical approach to process definition and modeling that can be used in a wide variety of situations.

The recommended approach for performing process representation consists of 15 tasks, each described in greater detail in the following sections:

1. Outline scope.

2. Sketch initial process architecture.

3. Identify, collect, and organize initial source material.

4. Revise scope.

5. Add supporting process models.

6. Add descriptive details to process assets (e.g., policies, activities, products, roles).

7. Package draft version.

8. Conduct external review.

9. Update process material (scope, architecture, models, and descriptions).

10. Pilot prerelease version with subset of target audience.

11. Perform final updates.

12. Conduct roll-out of final release.

13. Collect, log, and take action on feedback.

14. On a process area basis, repeat steps 1 through 13.

15. On a temporal basis, repeat steps 1 through 14.

To facilitate the explanation of concepts, various examples that follow use a variation of a peer review process. These examples elaborate a review process that is loosely based on the Fagan formal inspection process (Fagan 1986). The primary objective of this section is to show you a reasonably complete example of how to use IPDM to define and improve your process. This section is **not** intended to detail an actual review process. The key objective is to show, as clearly as possible, key aspects of IPDM and to do so by an internally consistent example.

3.2.1 Step 1: Outline Scope

Before embarking on defining or improving a process, explicitly define the scope, or boundaries, of the target process (Figure 3-2). The boundary of a process is its interface to the external world and is described in terms of the products that flow into the process, the products that flow out of the process, the resources necessary to support the process, and the constraints imposed on that process from external sources.

Therefore, a good way to start is to develop a list of all the products created by the process to be defined (all process outputs) and all of the products needed to perform the process (all process inputs). The process is operationally defined as the sum of all the activities required to produce the output products from the input products. Figure 3-3 shows an example. At this level, the process to be defined is always represented as a single "activity." Decomposition of the process is deferred until after the required external input and external output products are defined.

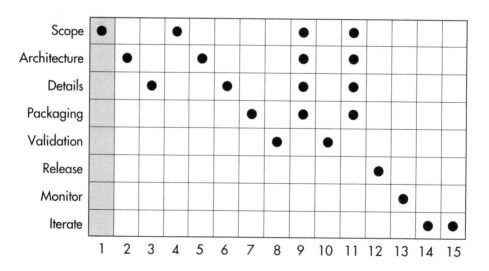

Figure 3-2. *IPDM Step 1*

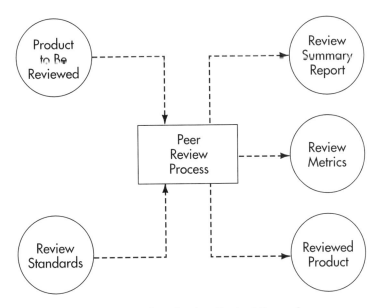

Figure 3-3. *Peer Review Context Example*

3.2.2 Step 2: Sketch Initial Process Architecture

Step 2 is to define the major activities believed to compose the process (Figure 3-4). Unless you are already familiar with the process, you will need to gather information from existing documentation and from interviews and other sources. Alternatively, if you are striving to define a new process, you may need to consult process experts, perform some simple process simulations, or do something else in order to construct the initial process decomposition. The goal is to identify three to ten activities that, in sum, represent the process. All aspects of the process must fit into one of the activities, and all of the external products must be produced by one or more of the activities.

This initial decomposition of the process into a small number of activities provides a structure for organizing the information you gather. The names of the activities identified are likely to change as you review your work with persons knowledgeable about the process and the terminology used in the area. You should try initially to limit the process decomposition to six major activities, because the model you are building will be much easier to understand if you can organize the process description into a few major activities with clearly defined relationships between them.

Once the names of the major activities have become relatively stable, the next step during information gathering is to build an indented list of activities. The purpose of the indentation is to reflect how higher-level activities can be broken down into lower-level

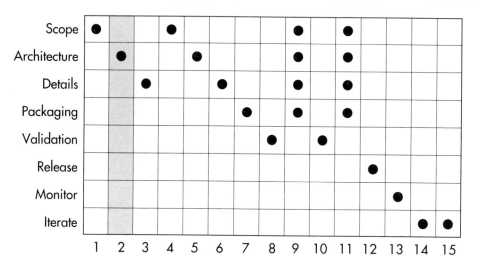

Figure 3-4. IPDM Step 2

activities or subactivities. For each item on this list, provide a unique identifier and a brief explanation of the activity's purpose and description.

At this stage, it is sufficient to attempt to define only the first two or three levels of the activity breakdown. The first, or highest, level defines the major activities occurring within the process. The second level defines the subactivities that make up each high-level activity. For example, subactivities of a project management activity might be:

- Perform cost-benefit analysis.

- Evaluate alternative solutions.

- Construct PERT chart.

At the third level, list the primary tasks that make up each activity. "Tasks" denote an activity that at this time is not further decomposed into subactivities. For example, the "evaluate alternative solutions" subactivity might decompose into three tasks:

1. Evaluate commercial solutions.

2. Evaluate alternative in-house solutions.

3. Evaluate consequences of doing nothing.

Of course, you may also decide that no further decomposition is necessary. For instance, you might decide to treat "perform cost-benefit analysis" and "construct PERT chart" as tasks.

For a peer review process, an indented list of the major activities may look like the following:

Peer Review Process

Inspection Activities
  Planning
  Overview
  Preparation
  Inspection Meeting
    Conduct Review
    Decide upon Reinspection
  Rework
  Follow-up
Causal Analysis

Products too can be described in terms of levels of composition, and an indented product list makes it easy to show the levels. For example, if an output is "Software Product," an example of an indented list is:

Software Product

Software Source
Software Object
Technical Documentation
  Administrator Guide
  User Guide

The indentation shows that the Software Product is composed of three major items: Software Source, Software Object, and Technical Documentation. Technical Documentation is composed of two guides. Initially you can use abstract names, such as "Software Product" for collections of related products, and later define lower levels of composition as more details are needed.

For a peer review process, the major products (both used or produced) are:

Peer Review Products

Product to Be Inspected
Review Memos
  *Invitation
  *Results
Review Metrics

This indented list follows the convention of indicating "specialization" children with a leading asterisk (i.e., there are two types of review memos: invitation memos and results memos). Additionally, you need to start identifying the key roles needed to perform the process (where role is defined as the set of one or more skills needed to perform the work adequately). This process is quite similar to that followed for activities and products. The major roles in the peer review example are:

> **Peer Review Roles**
>
> Review Team
>   Moderator
>   Scribe
>   Reader
>   Inspectors (are...)
>   *Key Inspector
>   *Regular Inspector
>   Developer
>   Review Coordinator

Once you have made (and edited) the indented lists you can reference them as you build one or more initial graphical models to help you and others understand the primary activities and the principal relationships that exist between them. As shown in Figure 3-5, an architectural model, the Peer Review process is composed of two primary activities: Inspection Activity and Causal Analysis. Inspection activity is composed of Planning, an optional Overview activity, Preparation, Inspection Meeting, an optional Rework activity, and Follow-up. The Inspection Meeting activity consists of two principal parts: a Review activity and a Decide activity, where the inspectors determine whether a reinspection is necessary. (Models and modeling conventions are discussed in more detail in Section 3.3.)

The indented lists provide the information needed to create architectural relationships. However, since lower levels of the indented list structure are likely to change as you gather more information, you should restrict the initial graphical models to one level higher than the lowest level of decomposition in the indented list. As you become more confident of the indented list decomposition, you can add detail to the graphical model.

3.2.3 Step 3: Identify, Collect, and Organize Initial Source Material

At this point, you have a clearly defined scope and an initial listing and decomposition of the major activities, products, and roles that compose the process. Use this information to gather any existing source material that describes how the process is actually (or intended to be) performed (Figure 3-6). Typically, you will find this material internal to your organization, but you may occasionally be able to reuse external sources also.

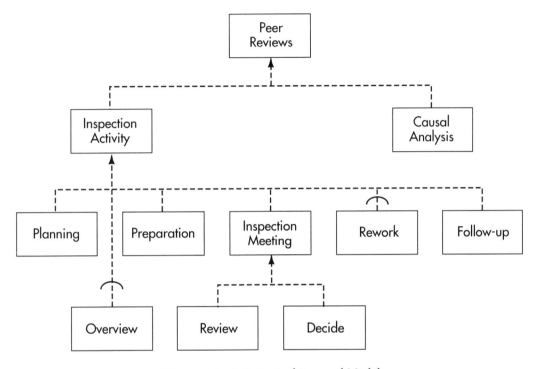

Figure 3-5. *Activity Architectural Model*

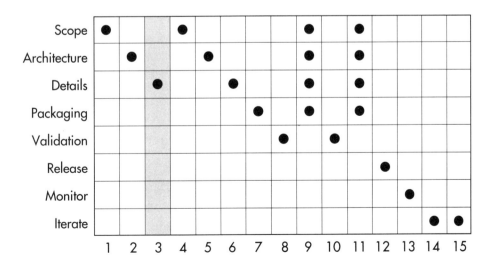

Figure 3-6. *IPDM Step 3*

Organize this material so that you are better able to see where, within the current process, you need to provide additional process information. You may need to provide this information because (1) the information did not previously exist, (2) the information exists but is obsolete, or (3) the information exists and is current, but part of the process is being changed.

One of the most important objectives of this step is to ensure that you make maximum use of (and reuse of) all available process-related material.

3.2.4 Step 4: Revise Scope

After you collect and organize existing process material, it is typical to find that some process subareas are larger than originally thought, others smaller, and some will be unexpectedly complicated, others simpler than expected. Consequently, it is important at this point to reexamine and, if appropriate, rescope the process being defined (Figure 3-7).

As part of this step you should reexamine and elaborate on the major internal products. An internal product differs from an external product (e.g., process inputs and outputs) by being an intermediate transformation between input products and output products. An internal product is a product produced by one activity and used by another activity toward producing an external product.

As you define the internal products, you may need to update the list of external products and the context diagram, if you created one. Updating is needed when a new external input is required so that an activity can produce an internal product, which eventually contributes

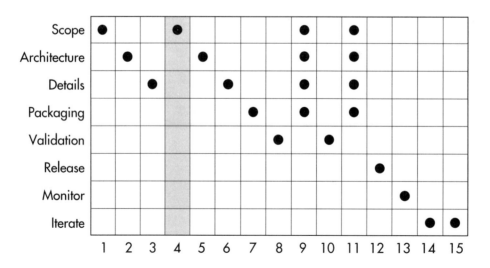

Figure 3-7. IPDM Step 4

to an external output. Any of these changes has the potential to affect your understanding and description of the scope of the process being defined.

After completing this step, you have identified the external products, the major activities composing the process, the internal products used and produced by the activities, and the most significant roles involved in performing the process. As information gathering continues and others review your work, you should expect iterations in the names of the activities, products, and roles, and in the composition of the indented lists, and the process scope as depicted in the Level 0 Context Diagram.

3.2.5 Step 5: Add Supporting Process Models

You are now well positioned to gather and organize a considerable amount of process details efficiently. However, to ensure you gather only what is needed and everything that is needed, this step consists of rapidly building additional process models (Figure 3-8). The purpose of these models is to indicate (1) how process objects are constructed, (2) how process objects relate to each other, and (3) how the process functions in time. These are referred to as architectural, interface, and behavioral models, respectively. (Details on modeling techniques are deferred until Section 3.3.)

Figure 3-9 shows a simple architectural view of the products involved in the Peer Review process. The three major products are: Product to Be Inspected, Memos, and Metrics. Also

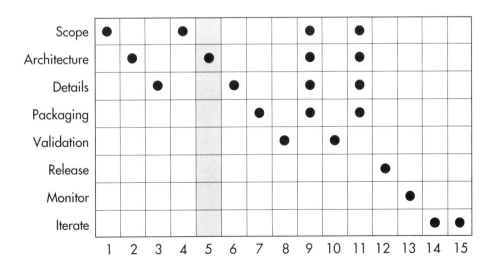

Figure 3-8. IPDM Step 5

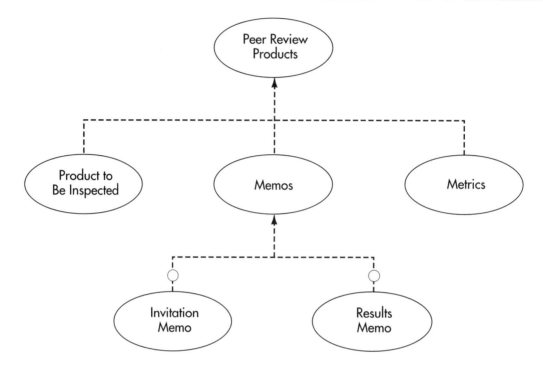

Figure 3-9. *Product Architectural Model*

shown is the fact that there are two types of memoranda: Invitation Memo and Results Memo.

Figure 3-10 shows an interface model of the high-level activities and products and resources that are involved in the Peer Review process. This model shows that Inspection activity needs the Product to Be Inspected, uses (or generates) Memos, and requires a Review Team. The Inspection activity generates a Metric product, which in turn is used by the Causal Analysis activity (which also requires a Review Team).

Figure 3-11 shows a slightly more detailed interface model of activities and products in the Peer Review process. Note that a detailed model does not necessarily show information seen at the higher level of abstraction. Typically, the two views shown simultaneously create too much clutter. Select the desired level of abstraction, and then concentrate on showing the objects and relationships at that level. This model shows that the Invitation Memo is generated by the Planning activity and used by the Overview, Preparation, and Inspection Meeting activities. This model also shows that the Product to Be Inspected originates from the external world, is needed in each of the activities, but is returned to the external world. Both the Inspection Meeting and the Follow-Up activities contribute to Metrics and the Results Memo.

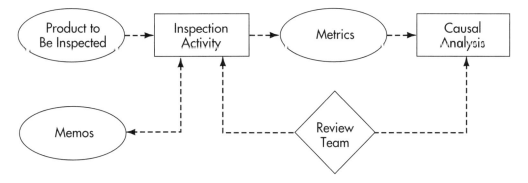

Figure 3-10. *High-Level Interface Model*

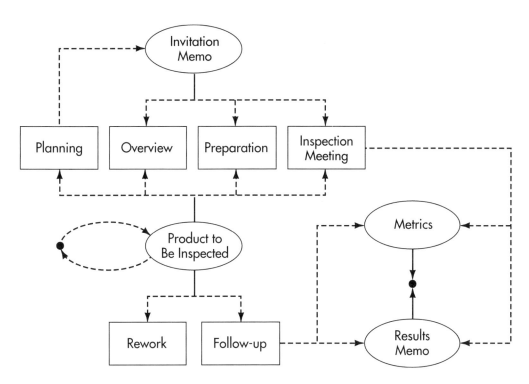

Figure 3-11. *Detailed Interface Model*

Figure 3-12 shows a behavioral model of the Inspection activity. This model shows that the review process starts with Planning; then either the Overview occurs, or the process may proceed straight into Preparation. After Preparation, the Inspection Meeting occurs.

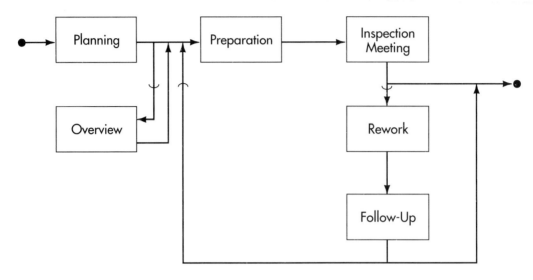

Figure 3-12. *Activity Behavioral Model*

Following the Inspection Meeting, the Peer Review process may be complete, or there may be a need for Rework. If the latter, then after the Rework is done, a Follow-up activity occurs. The Follow-up activity may be the last activity of the Review process; or if a reinspection is necessary, then the process loops back to the Preparation activity.

These are simple diagrams that omit many details. However, even diagrams like this can help you quickly communicate to others the primary process objects in your model and how those objects relate to each other.

3.2.6 Step 6: Add Descriptive Details to Process Assets

This step consists of determining exactly what you need to describe the important attributes of each type of process object (activity, product, and role) (Figure 3-13). For example, if you are following the ETVX paradigm, you will want to, at a minimum, define activities in terms of their entry conditions, the tasks of which are composed, validation, and exit conditions. (A detailed discussion of process object attributes and their use is presented in Chapter 5.) The term template is used to describe the set of attributes identified as important for a type of process object. The template may be, literally, a form that you fill in to provide the necessary information for a type of process object.

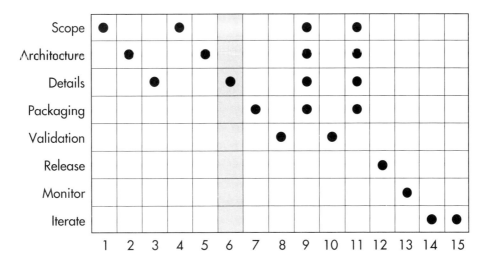

Figure 3-13. *IPDM Step 6*

3.2.6.1 Detail Activities

To start, detail any activity hierarchies by documenting whether an activity has been decomposed on the indented list into subactivities or tasks. All subactivities, by definition, have one or more parent activities. Based on the activity hierarchy represented in the indented list, add information to the activity description forms (or templates) about child and parent activities. Detail the two-way relationships for all activities (unless you are capturing process information using an information management system that automatically establishes reverse relationships). Use any available architectural models as aid in documenting parent and child relationships on the forms or templates.

Next, document all products generated or used by the activity. Higher-level activities typically reference higher-level products, and tasks reference lower-level or final products. If meaningful, also indicate whether a given product, within a given activity, is required or optional. The graphical model can help you confirm that you have captured all the relationships. If you discover additional relationships during this task, update the graphical model as appropriate.

Depending on what information is desired in your activity template, you might next document activity entry criteria. If so, for each activity, define the entry criteria unless the default entry criterion (the availability of each of the specified input products) is applicable. If only a subset of the input products is required for the activity to begin, the entry criteria should define the subset. The entry criteria can be defined in natural language, making reference to information such as whether other activities have been completed, or are underway.

The least error-prone approach is to start with the high-level activities, since the entry criterion for a subactivity is usually a reflection of the entry criteria of its parent. As the entry criteria are defined, ensure that they are consistent with the implications of the graphical models. If need be, update or alter the graphical model as insights are gained from ongoing analysis and the effort of filling in the templates.

Next, be sure to describe the internal processes within each activity. An activity's internal process is the principal description of the work that characterizes it. This description is done in terms appropriate to the abstraction level of the activity. Generally, describe what the activity is and/or how it is performed.

If there are constraints on how the internal process is done, describe them, for now, in natural language. An example of such a constraint is the need to follow a certain government standard in performing the activity. It may be useful to describe these constraints later using a more formal approach, including explicit construction and use of constraint templates.

For activities, you will likely also need to define exit criteria. For each activity, define the exit criteria, unless the default exit criteria (the production of each of the specified output products) is applicable. Other criteria may need to be met for the activity to be complete (i.e., a quality assurance [QA] review has also been satisfactorily completed). The exit criteria can be defined in natural language, making reference to information such as whether other activities have been completed.

At this point, you have described the activities in detail. The next step is to produce an equivalent level of detail in the product templates.

3.2.6.2 Detail Products and Roles

Similar to what you did for activities, you need to identify product hierarchies. Document the parent-child relationships between high-level products and the subproducts of which they are composed. These relationships will closely follow the indentation levels in the product indented list. The graphical model is also a useful reference (specifically, product architectural relationships, including both inclusion and specialization).

If you have need for very detailed process information (such as is needed to support process simulation or automated enactment), you will likely need to identify product-specific states. For example, a design document might have states such as "being drafted," "in review," "awaiting design inspection," "being updated," "completed," or "approved by QA." The state information can be used to make the internal processing descriptions of activities more precise, as well as being used in formulating entry and exit criteria.

Be cautious, however. Defining and maintaining product state information can be very time-consuming and should not be done unless you are certain how you will use the state information and that the benefits derived will justify the effort. Generally strive for the fewest number of states needed to support the model. For each product description, add only those states that are necessary or useful for defining relationships between the product and activities.

If you have explicitly defined products and their corresponding states, you may want to upgrade the internal process documentation within each activity to include references to the states of products. This can be especially useful for representing the review or quality assurance phases of a particular activity. Similarly, you may want to update entry and exit criteria to include product state references.

As with activities and products, document the set of information needed to describe each role on the indented list. Start with architectural or parent-child relationships. Keep in mind that architectural relations are of two types.

3.2.7 Step 7: Package Draft Version

A common mistake made by people involved in process improvement is to allow "ease of maintenance" to interfere with "ease of use." When process information is intended to be distributed to a target audience, that information must be packaged and presented in a manner that facilitates efficient and effective use by the intended audience (Figure 3-14). Consequently,

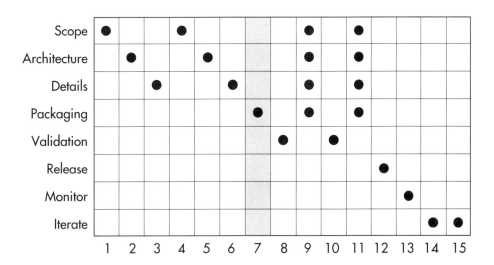

Figure 3-14. IPDM Step 7

complex or busy diagrams typically do not work; poorly organized descriptive text typically does not work; database dumps typically do not work. Instead, if you intend to produce, for example, a training manual from your process information, then you must repackage the process information so that it looks like, and is organized like, a training manual.

Following is a brief example of repackaging process information so that it looks and reads like a typical process specification. For space considerations, only a few pages are shown.

PEER REVIEW PROCESS

The technical office has decided that the peer review process used internally will be a variant of the Fagan formal inspection method. Comments and recommendations for improving either this material in particular, or the peer review process in general, should be forwarded through your local SEPG representative.

OVERVIEW OF PEER REVIEW PROCESS

The inspection method is one technique for the static verification of an artifact. Developed by Michael E. Fagan of IBM (Fagan 1986), the primary objective of this method is to detect defects in an artifact in an efficient and effective manner. Frequently referred to as a "formal inspection," you can use this method to verify any artifact generated during the development process, although considerable focus has been given to applying this method to preliminary design, detailed design, and code artifacts.

The inspection method consists of well-defined roles and activity stages. Associated with the roles are specific responsibilities. Additionally, entrance and exit criteria and objectives for each activity stage and mechanisms for recording and reporting defects ensure consistent application of this method.

The efficiency of this approach depends on focusing the participants on the overall objective of the method: defect detection. The effectiveness of this method depends on proper training of the participants and commitment by management to adhere to the prescribed process.

You can use the inspection method to verify any artifact generated during the development process. This section, however, states the specific purpose for preliminary design, detailed design, and code inspections.

During the preliminary design phase, hold preliminary design inspections to inspect the design documentation to verify that the requirements are satisfied and that the product will be maintainable, adaptable, and of high quality.

During the detailed design phase, hold detailed design inspections to inspect the design documentation to verify that the design has been refined correctly, is defined to a level that allows coding to begin, and satisfies assigned product requirements. Inspect the design to ensure that it is maintainable, adaptable, and of high quality.

During the implementation phase, hold code inspections to inspect the code to verify that it implements the detailed design correctly and completely.

The project team must baseline all reference material (specifications, requirements, documents) prior to the inspection meeting. For example, a preliminary design inspection cannot be held until the team has baselined the requirements. An example of a requirements specification document is a system requirements specification (SRS).

PEER REVIEW CRITERIA AND PROCESS

Entry Criteria

The author or project manager has selected a trained moderator for the preliminary design, detailed design, or code inspection.

The moderator has agreed to moderate the indicated inspection.

The moderator has been notified by the author that the preliminary design, detailed design, or code is completed, baselined, and ready for examination.

Internal Process

There are seven parts to the inspection process. Six of these parts are required: planning, preparation, inspection, causal analysis, rework, and follow-up. The optional part is the overview.

Exit Criteria

The Inspection Close Memo has been completed and distributed.

Invariants

The product being inspected continues to have purpose.

PEER REVIEW PROCESS-RELATED PRODUCTS

Inspection Input Product

    This is the product, item, or artifact to be inspected.

    The Inspection Input Product is needed before starting this activity.

    This activity leaves the Inspection Input Product unchanged.

    This is a required product.

Review Memos

    This product is the set of memorandums used to support the inspection process.

    This product is needed sometime after the activity has started.

    This product is created by this activity.

    This is a recommended product, but you have the option to apply for a waiver.

Review Metrics

    This is a hard-copy report summarizing the inspection results.

    This product is produced before the activity can be considered complete.

    This product is created by this activity.

    This is a required product.

PEER REVIEW PROCESS-RELATED ROLES

Peer Review Team

    The Peer Review Team participates in and is responsible for all phases of the Peer Review Process.

    This role is needed sometime after the activity has started.

    This is a required role.

Review Coordinator

    Review coordinators are responsible for organizing and overseeing reviews.

    The review coordinator role is needed before starting this activity.

    This is a required role.

PEER REVIEW PROCESS SUBACTIVITIES
    1.0 Activity Name: Inspection Planning

OVERVIEW OF INSPECTION PLANNING
During the planning stage, the author (i.e., owner) gives a copy of the material to be inspected to the moderator, who verifies the inspection readiness of the artifact. The moderator typically completes this assessment by using an entry criteria checklist suitable for the artifact type being inspected. If the artifact is ready to be inspected, the moderator and the author of the artifact identify relevant reference material, a checklist of likely defects (i.e., a preparation checklist), the participants and their respective roles, and the inspection schedule. The moderator generates the preparation checklist, which is suitable for the artifact type being inspected, by modifying a generic checklist.

The moderator uses planning guidelines, suitable for the artifact type being inspected, to aid in determining the inspection schedule. These guidelines include limiting the length of a single inspection meeting to 2 hours and not scheduling more than 4 hours per day to inspection activities. The moderator can derive guidelines to determine the duration of the overview, preparation, and inspection meeting activities from the planning criteria and process.

INSPECTION PLANNING CRITERIA AND PROCESS
Entry Criteria
The author submits a completed entry criteria checklist with the inspection package to the moderator. Refer to the appropriate procedure for the details of the entrance criteria checklists.

Internal Process
The moderator examines the materials to determine:

- The correct level of detail.

- Whether it is an appropriate amount to inspect.

- The availability of appropriate reference documents.

The moderator calculates the time required for the overview meeting, preparation time, and inspection meeting by dividing the size of the document to be inspected, in pages, or the code to be inspected, in lines of code, by the following estimates (these estimates are based on data related to an inspection process used in another organization and will be revised as data are collected):

- **Overview.** An overview should be limited to a single 2-hour meeting. If an overview longer than 2 hours is indicated by the length of the material, the moderator and the author should examine the material to divide it into separate inspection pieces. If the material indicates that an overview can be completed in a half-hour or less, the overview can be held at the beginning of the inspection meeting.

- **Preparation.** An estimate for preparation rates for preliminary design material is 12 to 15 pages per hour; for detailed design material, 8 to 12 pages per hour; and for code, 200 noncomment source statements per hour.

- **Inspection.** An estimate for inspection rates for preliminary design material is 10 to 12 pages per hour; for detailed design material, 8 to 10 pages per hour; and for code, 100 to 150 noncomment source statements per hour.

The moderator, project manager, or author contacts the inspection participants, tells them what is expected, and solicits available dates.

If an overview meeting is desired, it is scheduled by the moderator.

The moderator schedules the inspection using the estimated inspection meeting time computed earlier. An inspection may require multiple meetings. The length of a single inspection meeting should not exceed 4 hours in a given day. For each 4-hour meeting, it should be organized into a 2-hour meeting, a half-hour break, and then the remaining 2 hours.

The moderator or author (with approval of the moderator) distributes the inspection package consisting of the reference and inspection materials to the participants after appending the following:

- The Inspection Invitation Memo, which identifies the type of inspection, time, location, time charge number, participants, and job assignments for the inspection.

- Trivial Error Log.

Exit Criteria

If an overview meeting is indicated, the overview meeting has been scheduled.

The inspection meeting has been scheduled.

The inspection package has been distributed to all inspection participants.

INSPECTION PLANNING-RELATED PRODUCTS

Review Metrics

This is a hard-copy report summarizing the inspection results.

This product is needed before starting this activity.

This product is left unchanged by this activity.

This is a required product.

Inspection Invitation Memorandum

This memorandum is used to inform participants of an upcoming inspection.

This product is needed before ending this activity.

This product is created by this activity.

This is a required product.

INSPECTION PLANNING-RELATED ROLES

Review Coordinator

Review coordinators are responsible for organizing and overseeing reviews.

The review coordinator role is needed before starting this activity.

This is a required role.

Moderator

The moderator manages the overall inspection process and ensures that the requirements and intent of the inspection method are met.

The moderator role is needed before starting this activity.

This is a required role.

Developer

The developer is the person currently responsible for working on a product.

The developer role is needed before starting this activity.

This is a suggested role; the role typically participates in this activity, but you may, at your own discretion, exclude this role.

[Remaining activities would be shown in a pattern similar or identical to the above.]

SUMMARY OF PEER REVIEW PROCESS

This method supports two types of tailoring. The first is tailoring of guidelines and checklists to create an inspection process that adheres to the method and is relevant to the organization. You must do this type of tailoring to ensure a valid inspection process. The second type of tailoring is to modify the inspection method. This type of tailoring is optional. Additionally, tailoring of the method is subject to the limitations described below. The following discussion presents the mandatory tailoring followed by the optional tailoring.

Use of the inspection method requires that your organization establish supporting mechanisms—for example: entry criteria checklists, preparation checklists, and reinspection criteria for each artifact type that will be inspected. Each of these must be tailored to the organization's goals and the specific artifact being inspected.

Your organization may also tailor the classification of the defects. Typically, you classify defects, at a minimum, by type and severity. You may also classify each defect by category (e.g., missing, wrong, extra).

Because the objective of the inspection method is to find defects early in an efficient and effective manner, the focus is clearly on defect detection. One approach to tailoring the method, therefore, is to remove the causal analysis stage. The results of the causal analysis activity are intended to improve the development process to prevent the defect from occurring in the future. This stage emphasizes defect prevention. For organizations introducing the inspection process, the initial focus is probably on defect detection. The causal analysis activity could then be added in the future.

A second type of optional tailoring is to combine multiple inspections into a single inspection. This situation seems more frequent when inspecting a software artifact. An example is a change that is small in scale. The author may want to consider combining the preliminary design and detailed design inspections. Guidelines for determining when multiple inspections could be combined are:

- Combine the preliminary design and detailed design inspections when an update is made to an existing module and the preliminary design is not affected.

- Combine the detailed design and code inspections when the detailed design is done at a very detailed level and is expressed in the target language.

The moderator should be certified to run an inspection. Certification should consist of a minimum of one day of training in the inspection process and the specific role of the moderator within that process. In addition, newly trained moderators should be observed by an experienced moderator for the first two or three inspections. Other participants in an inspection should be given a 1-hour overview of the inspection process.

3.2.8 Step 8: Conduct External Review

At this point you have a process model and supporting details that describe the important activities products, and roles that form the process. Before proceeding further you should verify the correctness and consistency of your models and details to the maximum extent possible (Figure 3-15).

One possible verification vehicle is to conduct a model walk-through for reviewers knowledgeable about the process. In the walk-through, the model developer leads the reviewers through each step of the process, answering questions and identifying errors and missing information. The graphical model, backed up by the descriptive forms or templates, is the basis for the walk-through.

Such walk-throughs should be occurring on an ongoing basis throughout the process improvement and process definition and modeling effort. At this step of the process, it becomes critical to involve external people—actual process end users—in the validation of your process work. Be sure to tell the external review team that the material represents work in progress and that all recommendations received from the reviewers will be carefully evaluated and appropriate updates made.

Additionally, ensure that you allow your reviewers adequate time to perform the review. Monitor their progress, and when you receive their comments, be sure the comments are carefully logged and archived.

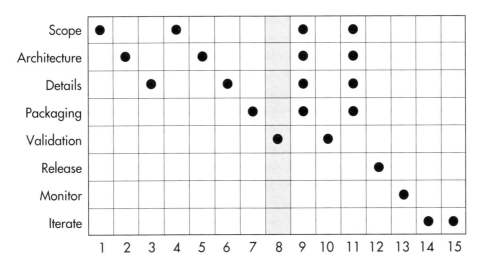

Figure 3-15. IPDM Step 8

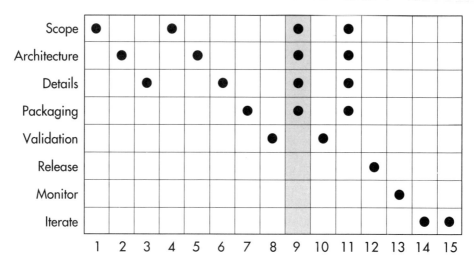

Figure 3-16. IPDM Step 9

3.2.9 Step 9: Update Process Material

This step is primarily a correction, clean-up, and simplification step (Figure 3-16). Keep in mind that anything that needs to be changed should be changed. For example, you may think the context diagram, and corresponding process scope, are perfectly appropriate for the process you are defining. However, the external reviewers may indicate something quite important is missing or, conversely, something unrelated was included. Be willing to make such changes. These people are representative of your actual audience, and if your work does not make sense to the target end users, it has no value.

More likely, the feedback you receive will address issues relating to details on the models or in the supporting descriptive information (or templates). As you strive to improve the quality and usability of this material, you will do so by continuing to improve:

- The fundamental model(s) underlying the process.

- The detailed information collected to document important attributes of process objects within the models.

- The selected subset of information chosen to represent the process to a specific audience.

- The organization and packaging of the subset of information.

In other words, you have many alternatives for improving quality, and it is not uncommon that the key difficulty end users have with process information is not with the information content itself but how that information was packaged and presented.

3.2.10 Step 10: Pilot Prerelease Version with Subset of Target Audience

At this point your process material has been through one or more internal walk-throughs, and at least one external review. Can you be confident that it is ready for release? Not quite. You have consensus that the process material should be ready for use, but that is not the same as validating that it truly is usable. The best way to gain insights into the usability of material is, of course, to use it for its intended purpose. This should be done via a pilot project (Figure 3-17).

A pilot project is one in which a relatively small percentage of your overall target audience uses the material you are producing to facilitate performing their work. Depending on organizational process improvement objectives (and constraints), the material might be used to disseminate and train the process, to analyze further and improve the process, or to plan and control the process. The material needs to be used as intended.

The purpose of this step is to collect from the pilot group insights into the strengths and weaknesses of the material and, if possible, recommendations for how it can be improved. Feedback indicating that "Section 2 is confusing and poorly organized" is not as useful as

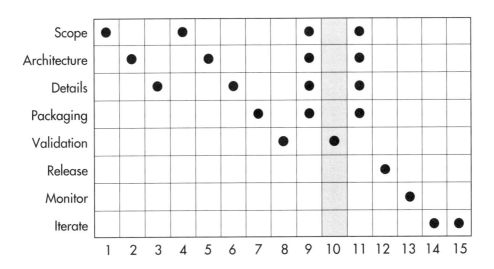

Figure 3-17. *IPDM Step 10*

"Section 2 can be made clearer if it is reorganized in the following way…" Be sure to communicate to the pilot project that recommendations are encouraged.

3.2.11 Step 11: Perform Final Updates

As with Step 9, the purpose of this step is to review all comments and recommendations received during the pilot project, and revise the scope of the process work, the process architecture, and other supporting models, process details, and the way in which the material is organized and packaged for use by the intended audience (Figure 3-18).

Generally, you can perform this work in parallel to the pilot project, updating information as feedback is received. To a limited degree, you can also redistribute updated information. However, if you elect to take this approach, be careful with configuration management of your process information. Clearly indicate versions and release dates on all material, and regularly check to ensure that all participants are using the latest material. Be especially careful not to make any material obsolete (by updating) before you have collected all comments relative to that material from all people on the pilot.

After performing the final updates, be sure to baseline the relevant process material and place it into configuration management.

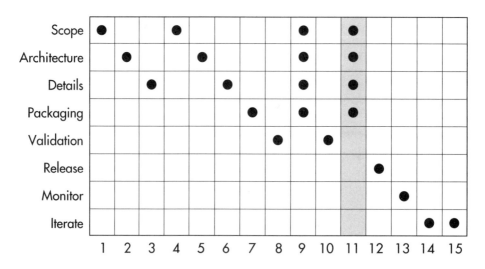

Figure 3-18. *IPDM Step 11*

3.2.12 Step 12: Conduct Roll-out of Final Release

Far too often process material is mass distributed to all affected parties. Generally, and especially with initial versions or major updates, it is important to be involved in the release and distribution of the process material. This is accomplished through roll-out meetings (Figure 3-19).

A roll-out meeting is relatively brief (ranging from 15 minutes to 1 hour), with the following items forming the majority of the agenda:

- Purpose of the new/revised process material.

- Motivation for developing and distributing the process material.

- Who was involved in developing the new material (be sure to highlight reviewers, participants on pilot projects, and anyone else who provided feedback, comments, support, or was otherwise involved in the effort).

- Brief overview of the process that was followed (again, emphasizing the involvement of end users).

- Overview of content.

- Guidelines on how best to use the new material.

- Instructions on how to contact the process group with comments and recommendations for improving the material.

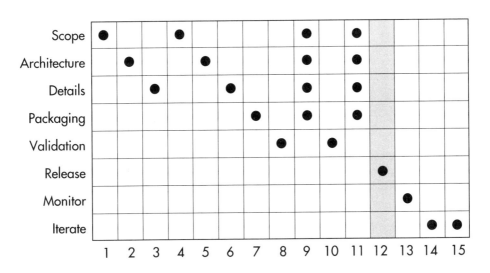

Figure 3-19. *IPDM Step 12*

The purpose of the roll-out meeting is not to provide training. If training is necessary, it should be handled separately (since generally not everyone will need training, but everyone should be invited to roll-out meetings). The primary objectives of the roll-out meeting are to (1) set end-user expectations, (2) communicate end-user benefit, and (3) ensure the end user knows that you are ready to listen and respond to all comments and recommendations.

3.2.13 Step 13: Collect, Log, And Take Action on Feedback

Process improvement cannot occur in isolation from those performing the process. Numerous studies have found that the people who are closest to the process are generally the first to become aware of process problems and generally have the best insights into how the problem can be addressed. Once you've fielded a new process, it is important to encourage feedback and to log all feedback received so that you may take action (Figure 3-20).

Often the appropriate action to take is "nothing, for now." This is why careful logging, archival, and tracking of process-related feedback is so important. It is best to avoid excessively churning the process by fielding numerous, successive, tiny updates. Instead, unless you have serious process issues requiring immediate correction, organize issues until the composite impact of addressing those issues is sufficient to field a major update to how the process is defined and performed.

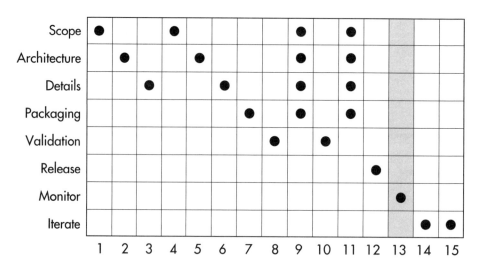

Figure 3-20. IPDM Step 13

3.2.14 Step 14: On a Process-Area Basis, Repeat Steps 1 Through 13

How do you know when a planned update in a given process area is, as presented in the prior step, "sufficiently major"? Careful process improvement and concurrent process representation is, as described here, a 15-step process. When you are ready to reexamine scope, revisit the process architecture, update the details, reconsider and potentially redo the packaging, submit the revisions to both internal and external reviews, conduct pilot projects, and so on, then you are ready for a major release. Conversely, if your impulse is to short-cut the sequence by leaving out one or more steps, then you should wait, and continue collecting, logging, and tracking feedback on the currently fielded process (Figure 3-21).

The process for conducting process improvement is in two key ways just like any other process: it needs to be well defined, and it needs to be practiced as defined. If your process improvement process isn't as good as you'd like it to be, fix the process, *but don't bypass it.*

3.2.15 Step 15: On a Temporal Basis, Repeat Steps 1 Through 14

Virtually all businesses find themselves subject to increasingly rapid rates of change. The rate of change particularly accelerates as a function of how technology intensive the business is. If you are producing high-technology products or rely extensively on high-technology tools and resources in the performance of your business, then the extreme

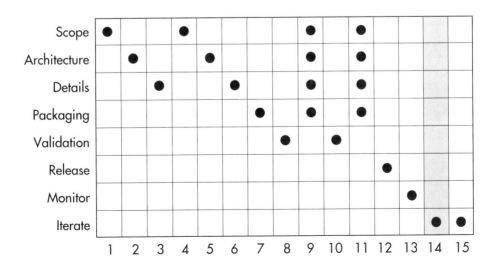

Figure 3-21. IPDM Step 14

volatility that characterizes high technology invariably translates into a need for you to reexamine and reoptimize your process continuously. The business that is first to capital- ize effectively on new opportunities made available by the latest developments in high technology usually takes market share from its competitors.

The prior step indicates that occasionally you need to reexamine and update the process in individual process areas. This step involves cyclically reexamining the entire system of processes that you have in place and determining whether there is now the need, or the opportunity, to achieve systemic or global process improvements (versus process-area or local process improvement) (Figure 3-22).

How often you invest the time and resources to reexamine your process at the systemic level is a function of how rapidly existing processes deteriorate due to changes in the mar- ketplace, business objectives, customer preferences, tools and technology, competitive products and practices, and other areas.

What is disconcerting for most organizations is the dawning realization that the cycle time needed to implement change is longer than the useful life span of the revised process. In other words, the world is changing faster than the organization's ability to respond effec- tively. There are many factors you can influence that directly improve the ability of your organization to be more agile and responsive within a rapidly changing world. These are discussed in detail in Chapter 4. The first step, however, is progressive scale-up of the num- ber and scope of the processes being monitored and improved. As this scale-up occurs, the use of process models becomes progressively more important.

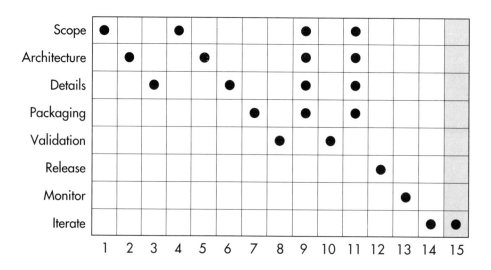

Figure 3-22. *IPDM Step 15*

3.3. PROCESS MODEL TYPES AND THEIR USAGE

Regardless of how careful you are in collecting, distributing, and managing process information—even if you are using process templates as your foundation—it quickly becomes impossible to remember all the information you have gathered, where you have placed it, and how you related it to other information. Graphical models are the primary means for restoring conceptual or high-level understanding. Arguably, there are a near-infinite number of process model types and a large body of published material explaining the details of various modeling methodologies.

For simplicity, IPDM distinguishes four major different types: architectural, interface, behavioral, and communication. The graphical conventions described in this section, intentionally kept simple, allow you quickly and easily to develop, analyze, and compare various models of your process.

It is strongly recommended that you use this or a similarly simple and fast approach while iterating through the creation and definition of your process assets. Once you are satisfied that your representation of the process is sufficient, you can import or export the relevant information to and from a database, for example, or use it as worksheets for developing graphical models that are more complex or labor intensive. This is typically more cost-effective than trying to maintain large, complicated, diagrams inside a difficult tool, especially during the early stages of process definition. During this time, increased understanding of the nature of and relationships between process assets results in repeatedly needing to make significant changes to your process models easily.

Another advantage to the conventions described here is that each node on a diagram should be used to represent one process object (i.e., a template or set of information that adequately describes an explicit activity, product, role, etc., at a given level of abstraction). This one-to-one relationship allows you to readily confirm consistency between your accumulating set of process details (on forms, templates, or captured within a database) and your graphical models of that information.

3.3.1 General Graphical Conventions

These graphical conventions emphasize the fact that there are process objects within your model, and there are relationships between those objects. Generally the three most important classes of process objects you need to diagram, and the symbols used to represent them, are:

- activities   ■
- products   ●
- roles   ◆

The four types of relationships are shown as:

- architectural   `- - - - - - - ->`

- interface   `- - - - - - ->`

- behavioral   `———————>`

- organizational reporting   `- - - - - ->`

These objects can be related to each other in a variety of ways. Relationships are shown using a variety of different lines, each indicating a different type of relationship. Sections 3.3.2 through 3.3.5 discuss details on the appearance and meaning of these relationships. Different lines and different arrow types are used so that you can build composite models that mix the type of information being communicated. However, there are disadvantages to doing so, as discussed in Section 3.3.6.

There are two other global conventions. First, any line that is struck by a small arc at either the source or the destination end of the line indicates an optional relationship. For example, a line pointing from a role to an activity indicates the role is needed by that activity. A small arc crossing that line by the arrowhead indicates the role is optional. If you have, for instance, several activities under a parent activity, and one or more of the child activities is optional, it usually creates less clutter to show the arc(s) at the source end of the line as it leaves the optional child(ren).

3.3.2 Architectural Relationships

Architectural models allow you to see how your process is constructed. For example, an activity may really consist of three subactivities, and one of those subactivities may itself have several still smaller tasks. Think of architectural models as a type of hierarchy chart. It shows how parts of things are built up into progressively larger parts. The fields "parent," "child," and "child type" directly facilitate constructing architectural models. Initially, you will likely need architectural models of three types of process objects: activities, products, and roles. Figure 3-23 shows an example of a process architectural model.

Architectural relations show parent-child relationships. There are two primary types of relationships used in building the process model:

1. **Composition.** Composition relations indicate that the parent object is composed of, or built from, all of the child objects. Figure 3-23 indicates that role (or team) A is made up of roles (or team members) B, C, and D.

2. **Specialization.** Specialization relations show that the parent has one of several different forms. In Figure 3-23, role D is shown to be either role E or role F. As an example, role D may indicate the role of an inspector, and roles E and F

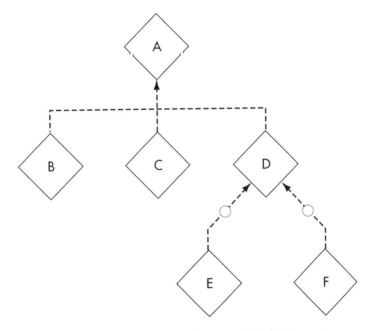

Figure 3-23. *A Process Architectural Model Example*

indicate that there are two types of inspectors: key inspectors and regular inspectors. The circle by the arrowhead indicates a specialization relation. The circle can also be placed at the source end of the arrow; this style is typically preferred if several arrows join into one.

3.3.3 Interface Relationships

Interface models communicate how activities, products, and roles are related within a process. The most common form of these models is information flow diagrams. These models are constructed by examining activity forms or templates for the information groups that show the products needed by and released by the various activities.

Figure 3-24 shows a variety of interface relationships (represented by dashed lines) and is interpreted as follows:

- Activity A1 needs both role R1 and role R2.

- Activity A1 always produces product P2, and sometimes ("optionally") produces product P1.

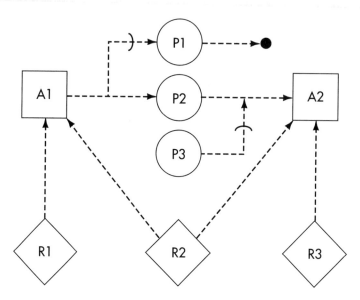

Figure 3-24. *A Process Interface Model Example*

- Activity A2 needs role R2 and role R3.

- Activity A2 requires product P2, and may optionally use product P3.

- Product P1, if it is produced, is sent to some external "sink" (such as might be shown on, or at least implied by, a level 0 context diagram).

It is clear that this figure does not necessarily tell you everything you want to know. For instance, once the product P2 is available, can the role R2 be shared between A1 and A2? Although this type of information can be found on or deduced from the templates, those details are lost in this particular diagram. However, adding more detail is not always the solution: cluttered diagrams quickly begin to be confusing.

With any diagram, you are deliberately eliminating details so that you may emphasize what you consider to be most important. With interface diagrams, the primary objective is to show, at an abstract level, how roles, products, and activities all coexist.

3.3.4 Organizational Reporting Relationships

Organizational models convey how the human resources within a process communicate with each other. Note that this is different from the "authority" structure implied by an architectural model of roles (that is, levels of authority). For instance, an architectural model of a division might show that a division manager has authority over project managers, each of whom has authority over several team leaders, who have authority over their respective teams. However, the project managers may have to report to someone in the quality assurance group and someone in the business or finance office. In this example, the quality assurance group does not have authority over the project leaders, but they do need periodic reports from those project leaders. This is the key difference between organizational models and architectural models of roles. On the role template, there are specific fields to capture information about who reports to a given role and to whom the given role reports. Figure 3-25 shows an example of a process reporting model.

Organizational relationships exist only between roles; they show, for any given role, who (or which roles) reports to it, and to whom this given role reports. Figure 3-25 tells us that role D is reported to by roles A, B, and C. It also shows that role D must report to role F and, optionally, to roles E and G.

If you suspect that a reporting relationship can also be conveyed using interface models showing project managers' passing reports to the configuration management group, you are correct. It is always the case that a body of process information can be modeled in a variety of ways. The key issues are what you are trying to communicate and which type of model best supports that type of communication. Process models, with the possible exception of automated enactment usage, are chiefly valuable as communication tools.

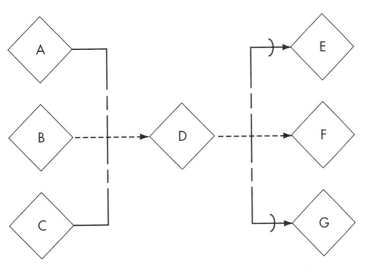

Figure 3-25. A Process Reporting Model Example

3.3.5 Behavioral Relationships

Behavioral models convey the sequencing of events in time and highlight process execution characteristics such as concurrent activities, alternative activities, and activity rendezvous. Entry criteria, internal process, exit criteria, and invariant information are the primary ways in which behavioral information is captured. Figure 3-26 shows an example of a process behavior model.

Behavior relationships are used to show the ordering (full or partial) of activities. Figure 3-26 shows several ways in which activities are arranged. The primary arrangements of interest are:

- Origination: What happens first.

- Sequence: When an activity is done, another may start.

- Selection: When an activity is done, one of several others may start.

- Iteration: When an activity is done, it may repeat or be part of a repeating series.

- Dispatch: When an activity is done, several may start.

- Rendezvous: When several activities are done, another may start.

- Release: When any one of several activities is done, another may start.

- Termination: What happens last.

The following list provides details on interpreting Figure 3-26:

- **Origination.** Origination is shown as a small, dark circle with an arrow going out to one or more activities. Activities A and E are both originating activities. This process begins with both A and E executing in parallel.

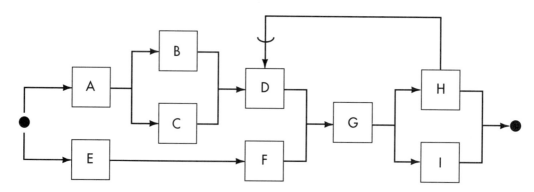

Figure 3-26. *A Process Behavior Model Example*

- **Sequence.** Sequence, in its simple form, is one activity following another. This is shown as activity F following E.

- **Selection.** Selection indicates that only one of the following activities may execute. For example, after activity A is done, either B or C may start but not both. To indicate selection, always use a single departing arrow; then branch for each of the possible following activities.

- **Iteration.** Iteration is shown by the arrow leaving activity H and pointing back to activity D. Note that this arrow has a small arc by the arrowhead pointing to D, indicating an optional relationship. In other words, there might be a need to return to H from D, but not always.

- **Dispatch.** Dispatch is shown by multiple lines leaving an activity, or starting node, arriving at different activities. The originating node indicates this activity starts with the dispatch (parallel activation) of A and E.

- **Rendezvous.** Rendezvous is shown by several lines, each separately arriving at an activity. This is shown as activity G waiting on both activity D and activity F to finish. Note that this brings together the work of A and E.

- **Release.** Release is indicated by several lines joining into one line, and then that one line going to an activity. When either activity B or C is done, activity D starts.

- **Termination.** Termination is shown by one or more arrows pointing to a small, dark circle. Consistent with the conventions just described, if several arrows each independently points to the terminal mark, it indicates that each of the activities must complete. If the arrows join before arriving at the terminal mark, then any one of the preceding activities serves as the final activity. Both H and I are potential terminal activities.

You can build behavioral models using these or numerous other modeling conventions from the information gathered on process object forms and templates. There is a general relationship between the type of models you build and the formality needed in your process descriptions. At lower tiers (1 and 2) your process information and relationships are comparatively less formal than what is required to build successful representations at higher tiers (5 and 6). A static behavioral diagram can be considerably less formal than an enactable behavioral model intended for use in automated process control.

3.3.6 Mixing Models

Because each of the roles has a different shape, and each of the relationships uses a different type of line, it is possible to build composite or overlay models that strive to show a variety of information and relations simultaneously. Generally, this should be avoided. However, if you want to combine two or more types of simple models, be sure to verify that the resulting hybrid actually improves communication and understanding. At all tiers, the goal is always to facilitate accuracy, clarity, and communication. Cluttered diagrams quickly become a hindrance, and they are labor intensive to maintain. The conventions presented in this section are specifically intended to help you build models with a minimum of effort that communicate a significant amount of process information.

3.4 SUMMARY

One of the most important characteristics of IPDM is its flexibility. Throughout this book we recommend you use some form of automated tool support—in particular, an information management system—for capturing and maintaining process data. A key reason is the extensive options provided by these environments. The examples in this chapter only hint at the almost unlimited flexibility you have in how you capture process information and how you can export that information for use by other software packages.

The next chapter temporarily departs from the how-to details of performing process representation and examines other critical aspects of performing process improvement successfully within your organization. In particular, issues relating to human factors are carefully explained.

Chapter

4

KEY ELEMENTS OF
PROCESS IMPROVEMENT

Having a successfully defined process consists of more than just having a set of process representations. To remain useful, these representations, especially those intended to guide practitioners, must be accepted, trained, performed, and evolved. In addition, they need to be of such quality that the organization's products and services are successful and result in the organization's having sustained success. Additionally, to have an SEI CMM defined process you need both to establish the process descriptions necessary to assess at SEI Level 3 and to have the integrated process trained, practiced, enforced, measured, and able to be improved though an institutionalized organizational process focus (Paulk et al. 1993).

Achieving a successful project- or organization-wide defined process is not easily or quickly accomplished. Typically, significant organizational and cultural change is involved. This chapter covers a number of the key issues in achieving organizational and engineering success: understanding change, introducing process definition and modeling into your organization, the use of metrics, process representations for training, and top-down versus bottom-up process representation.

This material was introduced in Chapter 2, and many of the concepts explained in this chapter have been previously introduced. The purpose here is to integrate earlier preliminary or basic material into the larger context of organizational change management and thereby give a more comprehensive and expanded treatment of these topics.

4.1 CHANGE

High-technology companies, and in particular software producers, are affected by rapidly changing markets; tight budgets; increasingly critical roles for software in competences and products; new customer and standards requirements on software suppliers; and new, expensive technology. Your organization may be motivated to define and improve its process due to a variety of forces affecting software development and maintenance: international competition, ISO 9000 compliance, the SEI levels of software process maturity, down- or right-sizing of computers and staff, corporate TQM programs, and the use of software and computing in strategic, new, competitive products and services. This results in a need for more powerful, reliable, flexible, standards-compliant, and less labor-intensive approaches to software engineering.

4.1.1 Organizational Change

Organizations differ widely in the ways they address process improvement. Some handle it as stressful episodes; others try to learn from each improvement but are poor at applying any lessons; and others treat process definition and improvement as a core competency with organizational structures, processes, and incentives aimed at maximizing their competitive advantage deriving from this area.

From this perspective, process improvement involves the managed exchange of information and resources both within your organization and with related, external organizations. Figure 4-1 shows a number of organizations and conditions that affect process improvement as well as the subsystems mentioned.

When an organization views process improvement as an ongoing function, organizational arrangements to handle technologies and process improvements may be instituted and improved. Each of these issues must be considered:

- **Strategic subsystem.** Does your organization have a business strategy, or does it simply react to whatever changes come along?

- **Technological subsystem.** Are the processes used to transform inputs into outputs standardized and institutionalized? Do the processes rigidify operations, or are they flexible? What types of technologies are being used?

- **Human/cultural subsystem.** What are the core values, behaviors, and unwritten rules that shape your organization's culture? What orientations do people bring to work? Are employees searching for challenge and involvement or simply working for money?

- **Structural subsystem.** Is your organization bureaucratic and hierarchical or matrix in structure? Are integrated product teams used?

- **Managerial subsystem.** Does the dominant managerial philosophy stress accountability and control (authoritarian) or encourage initiative and enterprise (democratic)? Does the organization stress innovation and risk taking?

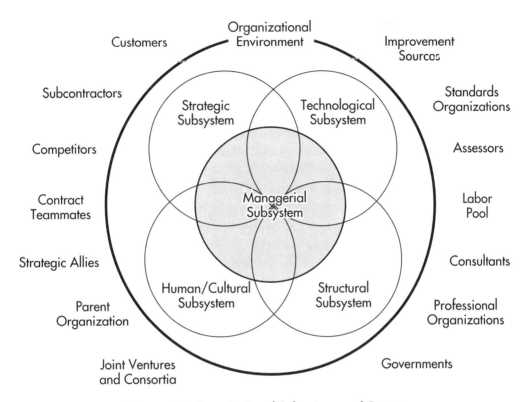

Figure 4-1. *Organizational Subsystems and Context*

- **External entities and relationships.** Do your processes mesh smoothly with your suppliers and customers? How do you assess and address customer satisfaction? Do you have mutually beneficial long-term relationships with technology sources? How do you compare to your current and future competitors? Do you exploit consortia?

4.1.2 Organizing for Software Process Improvement

A typical organizational structure recommended for software process improvement has a software steering committee that coordinates, supports, and guides one or more SEPGs, which in turn create and support process action teams (PATs) that do various process improvement tasks and participate in piloting new methodologies, techniques, and tools. This example structure will vary by organization, but the roles enumerated in Section 4.1.3 will likely be common regardless of your overall organizational structure.

4.1.3 Roles in Organizational Change

Staff at any level in your organization can play one or more of the following roles in process improvement:

- **Sponsor.** This person possesses sufficient authority or influence to initiate resource commitment for process improvement (*authorizing sponsor*) or reinforce process improvement efforts at the local level (*reinforcing sponsor*). Both authorizing and reinforcing sponsors continually legitimize and demonstrate ownership and commitment to process improvement. The departure or unavailability of sponsors could jeopardize the success of an improvement activity or group.

  The authorizing sponsor is usually the senior manager of the organization and often serves as the chairperson of the software steering committee. Reinforcing sponsors are typically at a middle manager level and are present within the software steering committee.

- **Change agent.** This person or team is empowered by sponsors to implement and facilitate process improvement throughout the organization. The SEPG and the PATs are considered change agents.

- **Champion.** This person advocates and publicly supports software process improvement in the organization but lacks the power to sanction it. A champion can be present at any and all levels of an organization; successful ones are usually respected for personal or technical leadership.

- **Process users.** This group of people implements the change and is the focus of the effort; they are expected to follow the process definition in the way they work and are therefore likely to change their behavior. Throughout the cycle of process improvement, everyone affected by the change will be changing some aspect of the way they work. Typically, process users are the people who develop the organization's software products and are commonly considered the technical staff.

Any of these roles may, at some time, be subject to change (changing some aspect of the way they work). Sponsors may need to change their communication style to stress better the importance of process improvement. Change agents may need to develop their interpersonal skills to build strong teams within the organization.

These roles will evolve and overlap during the process improvement program. For example, a sponsor may start out as a subject of the change effort. The champion influences this manager to become an authorizing sponsor. Upon authorizing the proposed change, the sponsor may champion the improvement on a larger scale and to other organizations.

4.1.4 Evolutionary Change Process

To be consistently successful, process definition efforts need to be part of a viable and well planned and -implemented process improvement effort. As introduced in Chapter 2, you can follow a cyclic or spiral process for process improvement. Though process improvement activities and their dates cannot be accurately predicted in detail far in advance, a well-structured and executable plan can be developed by considering a set of core activities you can plan and execute in an iterative manner (Software Productivity Consortium 1993a). Figure 4-2 presents an overview of this process. The key steps are:

1. **Understand context.** Understand the current context, including support for improvement, viable alternative strategies, and process.

2. **Analyze risks and select strategy.** Analyze risks and select a strategy for implementation.

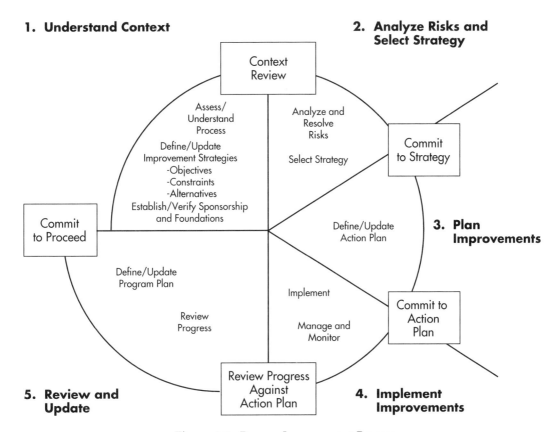

Figure 4-2. Process Improvement Process

3. **Plan improvements.** Plan the improvements for this cycle.

4. **Implement improvements.** Implement the improvements according to the plan.

5. **Review and update.** Review progress and update overall plans.

Advocating, planning, performing, reviewing, and managing process engineering and process definition are involved in potentially all of these activities, but the process definition activities concentrated on elsewhere in this guidebook fit mainly into the Implement activity as part of carrying out an action plan.

4.1.5 Starting with the Evolutionary Spiral Process

The evolutionary spiral process (ESP) provides a starting place for a sophisticated, modern process. You should find it useful particularly if you have requirements for a substantial amount of variation and tailoring. It also is a good source of risk management methods if you want only them, and it contains activity definition outlines and artifact and role lists that may be useful as a starting point.

To date, most process models have been tied to a specific life-cycle model, to the point that it is very difficult to distinguish the process from the life cycle. Another problem to tying the life-cycle perspective completely to process models is that life-cycle representations are linear and do not highlight the impact of feedback and iteration. A third problem arises when projects do not define a process model that would best suit their unique situation but rather attempt to use a model that is mismatched to project objectives and constraints because it is readily available or required by the customer. On the other hand, it is often difficult and overly constraining to define a model that is best suited to the project's objectives and constraints at the beginning of a project without knowing what surprises are in store as the project progresses.

The ESP model attempts to resolve these difficulties by providing a process model that:

- Is intentionally not tied to a specific life cycle.

- Can be used to define and evolve a life cycle that will best meet project-unique objectives and constraints.

- Will help incrementally generate the development process used to reach the life-cycle states.

The ESP model is based on the spiral model, originally developed by Boehm (1989, 1992) to address the known problems in more conventional, primarily waterfall, life-cycle models. The spiral model explicitly incorporates the management steps missing from most of the earlier models. It permits its users to avoid the automatic adoption of one-size-fits-all processes and eliminates the lock-step or linear progression of stages characteristic of the earlier models.

The conceptual ESP model, shown in Figure 4-3, is essentially a management model. It is described by five main steps and several specific product and process management activities that can be used in conjunction with any life-cycle model. A cycle starts in the upper left quadrant with the step to determine objectives, alternatives, and constraints; then it moves clockwise. In addition, you can follow the ESP model activities to determine a life-cycle alternative that will adequately address your objectives and constraints, incorporate the life cycle into the model, and subsequently evolve the life cycle as product development proceeds and objectives and constraints change.

The ESP model is meant to be repeated using the knowledge gained and lessons learned from the previous cycles; that is, you traverse all five steps of the ESP model one cycle at a

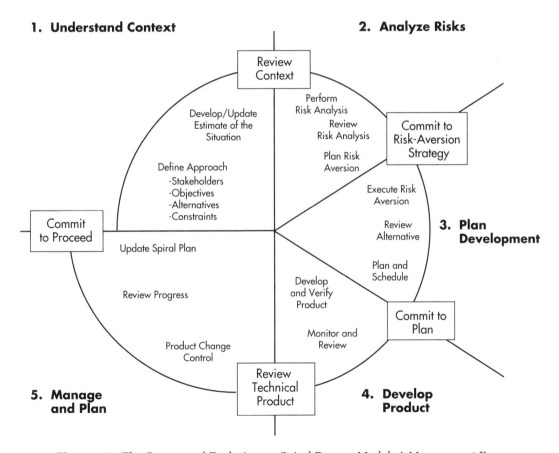

Figure 4-3. *The Conceptual Evolutionary Spiral Process Model: A Management Focus*

time. A cycle is a complete traversal of all five steps that, when completed, matures the product by the amount defined in cycle-specific objectives and success criteria. A spiral is one or more cycles that, when combined, accomplish a specific objective, such as complete a project, product, work product, or other major milestone. A spiral may represent the complete life cycle or may include only the activities necessary to meet one or more of the life-cycle states.

By identifying and incorporating a specific life-cycle model into the conceptual ESP model, you can engineer a process model specific to your situation. When the problem is well understood, you may be able to apply the waterfall, or top-down, approach successfully, elaborating all requirements before starting design, completing the design before writing any code, and finishing the code before integration and test. However, you may not have enough details to write the correct requirements until you have developed a prototype or performed some preliminary design. You almost guarantee some amount of rework if you adhere strictly to the top-down sequence. In this case, you may engineer a process model, such as the one shown in Figure 4-4, that permits a more opportunistic schedule for product development because it allows you to postpone some key requirements decisions where you might otherwise have been forced to make a choice with insufficient knowledge.

In the sample ESP model shown in Figure 4-4, you could have defined the life cycle in the first cycle and then updated the model to show the specific product life-cycle states and supporting activities in cycles 2 through 4. As the spiral progresses, you can evolve the process model to accommodate changing objectives and constraints, identified risks, and lessons learned. This example is only one possible elaboration of the spiral. Each project can have a customized spiral(s) to fit its situation.

Regardless of whether you are defining project-level or organizational-level processes, an iterative, spiral approach directly facilitates building and validating process descriptions that progressively improve in terms of depth, breadth, and maturity.

4.2 INTRODUCING PROCESS DEFINITION INTO YOUR ORGANIZATION

An additional challenge in implementing successful process improvement is introducing the concept and practice into an organization that has not previously understood the value of developing and maintaining a well-defined process. Successful transfer of process definition activities into your organization depends on getting people to change—or, at least, formally document and control changes in—the way they work. Usually you cannot be successful at getting people to change just by mandating it or by handing them a new process definition and expecting them to use it. You have to show them, in detail, how the change will affect their work in the short and long term, ensure that they are motivated to change, and then support them throughout the transfer. Figure 4-5 shows factors that, if implemented, will improve your chances of successfully transferring a process definition into use.

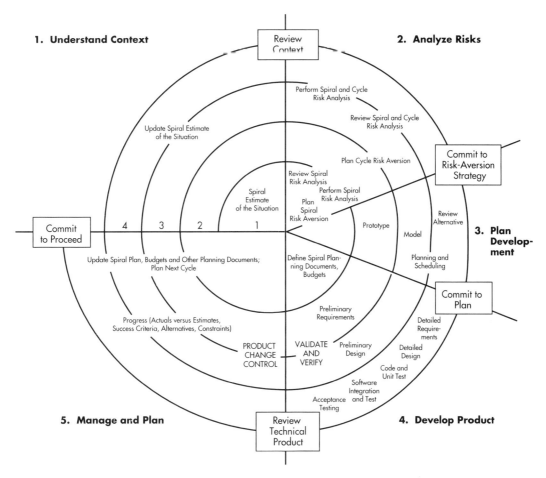

Figure 4-4. *An Elaborated Evolutionary Spiral Process Model: A Complete Process Focus*

4.2.1 Technology Transfer

The key challenge in process definition is not defining processes but persuading people to accept and comply with new processes. Although this issue was introduced, and some general guidelines provided, in Chapter 3, you need to realize that technology transfer, or the insertion of new processes, is a large field and can be a special study unto itself (Software Productivity Consortium 1993b). Generally, however, you should consider the following guidance when starting or performing technology transfer:

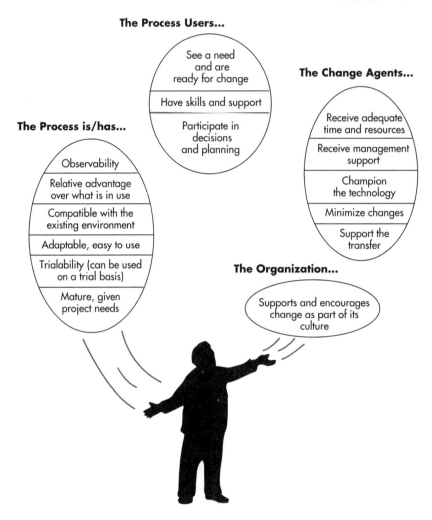

Figure 4-5 *Success Factors in Process Transfer*

- **Needed commitment.** Your sponsors need to understand that if they attempt a transfer and fail, they incur costs (adapted from Implementation Management Associates 1992). There are short-term costs that are direct (e.g., wasted resources and failure to achieve a stated business objective) and indirect (e.g., staff morale suffers because they may have invested their own time and energy into a failed transfer). There are long-term costs too. If management commits to something that fails, staff will potentially have a lower confidence in management's leadership ability and will increase their resistance to the next transfer they are asked to support. So as not to incur these costs, your sponsors need to make sure they support the transfer throughout the entire process. They cannot just give it lip-service, expect it to succeed, and not expect any repercussions when it fails. If there is any doubt about whether you will receive ongoing support, you should get new sponsors, or delay the transfer until the support is received; otherwise you will fail.

- **Scope.** Establishing the scope of the process definition effort needs careful consideration, particularly at the beginning. Among the factors to consider are your purposes (goals, objectives, motivations), constraints, alternatives, risks, opportunities, existing situation and plans, time frame, cost and benefits, and the exact products. In addition to organizational scope and users, you need to address depth, generality, adaptability, and integration.

- **Cost and schedule.** Most technology transfers are expensive. If you are tight on resources, you can possibly make up for it in the beginning by stretching out your schedule, but there will come a time when management will have to provide adequate resources. If you are limited on time and resources (and cannot change the situation or scale back to fit), the best guidance is to delay the transfer until your situation improves.

- **Timing.** For the most part, organizations can perform work only when they have a stable environment. If at all possible, time the transfer to occur at the beginning of an effort or at a major transition point when people are able to absorb changes better. It is nearly impossible to get an ongoing project to change, especially in the middle of schedule and resource crunches. Process improvement, and therefore definition and transfer of processes into use, is best done by a series of cycles rather than everything, everywhere at once.

- **Activity duration.** Perform the transfer activities as rapidly as possible by performing activities and tasks concurrently. This might mean trading detail, elegance, and perfection (but not effective usability) for speed.

- **Cycle duration.** The length of a cycle will be dependent on the situation. However, you can use the following rules of thumb when planning a cycle: the more people involved in the current cycle, the shorter the cycle should be because of the higher probability that risks will occur; and the more comfortable your organization is with the activities planned for the cycle (e.g., training), the longer the cycle can be because your organization already knows how to mitigate most of the risks. One possibility is to time the cycles to correlate to your reporting cycle; for example, if management wants to see a progress report every 3 months, then you can time your cycles to be approximately 3 months in length.

- **Resources.** In general, transferring in a tool alone will take the least amount of resources, transferring in a method alone will take more resources, transferring in a tool and associated method together will take even more resources, and transferring in a system or software development life-cycle process will take the most resources. This is due to the increasing levels of impact on existing practices of each technology type.

4.2.2 Understand Your Purposes and Their Implications

Like any other systems or software engineering effort, many of the potentially serious problems in achieving a defined process are related to requirements. What are the goals and their relative importance? Who are the stakeholders, and what are their concerns? What are the success criteria and measures? Do the resources fit the requirements? What requirements have the greatest risks? These are all typical questions that are important here. Your requirements for the process definition-related efforts exist in a context of organizational requirements.

Achieving a clear, shared, explicit statement of the objectives that reflect your needs in a particular situation is a key to success. Objectives can involve understanding (particularly understanding the requirements a process must meet), having an as-is definition, or improving. Process improvement efforts vary in scope and goals.

The scope of organizational objectives can be of five kinds (adapted from Venkatraman 1991): (1) localized improvements, (2) improvement integrated internally across organization, (3) business process redesign, (4) business network redesign including suppliers, customers, and others, and (5) business scope redefinition, where new process and technology are used to break out and change the organization's mission, scope, markets, and products. Your initial definition effort is more likely to to be successful the earlier it is on this list of kinds.

If your situation is typical, it will be somewhat mixed, with objectives varying for different parts of the definition(s). For some part, say, configuration management, you may be satisfied with how this is done in a portion of your organization and want to capture these satisfactory internal example processes that you will then propagate. For other parts, your management's instructions may be, "We are lousy at that. Do not study how we do it now. Define us a good process." Of course, the greater the fraction that falls in the first category, the easier introduction should be.

Identify the symptoms that your sponsor, users, and others most want to see change. Project overruns, shipped defects, excessive integration costs, time-to-market, SEI CMM level: what is it that will make it a success in their eyes? You will probably need to do some root cause analysis to go from symptoms to process causes.

Process definition can be used to help many kinds of activities. Figure 4-6 lists many uses of definitions. As shown, process definitions are used for anything from marketing, through process engineering and organizational change, to ISO 9000 certification. Use this list of process definition uses to remind you of those that are important to you.

4.2.3 Process Definition and Modeling Staff

When introducing or expanding a process definition and modeling effort, you must determine which roles are necessary for supporting the work and what types of skills are desirable for people performing those roles. Arguably, three to five matrixed engineers and one matrixed manager are necessary for establishing a process representation (definition and modeling) program. Because some training is involved, there is too much risk in training only one person and then having the entire program depend on the efforts and availability of that person. In principle, it is better to have more people contributing smaller amounts of their time than to have fewer people contributing significant amounts of time. Once a program is well underway, it is ideal to have one or more people work their way into full-time responsibilities as process engineers.

The preferred candidates for such work are those who have a process-oriented background. This group includes people who have had experience in systems analysis and design. These individuals have had considerable exposure to process control at a systemic

Marketing	Understanding	Institutionalization	Productivity
Transferring	Design	Cultural Change	Predictability
Selection	Definition	TQM	Time-to-Market
Trial	Analysis	Process Improvement	Cost Lowering
Tailoring	Reasoning	Process Reengineering	Quality Improvement
Training	Review	Tool Development	Standardization
Learning	Integration	Environment Development	Vendor Evaluation
Remembering	Change	Team Building	SEI CMM Assessment
Performance	Reuse	Organizational Unity	Certification (e.g., ISO 9000)
Planning	Traceability	Multiorganization Coordination	
Measurement	Communication		
Management	Knowledge Capture		
Quality Assurance	Shared View		

Figure 4-6 *Uses of Process Definitions*

level. Also included are individuals who may have received exposure to systemic process issues through involvement with TQM, process assessment efforts, and similar activities.

The learning curve involved in becoming proficient in IPDM is comparatively nominal, so the benefits of having several people trained and potentially available (as matrixed resources) for process representation efforts are relatively low cost and low risk. This is especially true when you consider the value derived from the increased variety of insights and experience.

The detailed process information captured on forms or templates can be used as a point of departure for alternative process representation notations such as ETVX, SADT, and Petri Nets. If such notations are one of the eventual goals of the process representation effort, it is highly advantageous to select process engineers partially as a function of whether they have a background in the alternative notation of choice. In all cases, using alternative notations for constructing process models is consistent with their use in constructing software models. Consequently, notation-specific skills previously acquired by process engineers can be applied to process representations using those notations.

Once you have identified who will be working as process engineers, the next step is to identify the first area to be defined. Your own process definition process can be a good example to learn on, but do not spend excessive resources or unreasonably delay the main work.

4.2.4 Guidelines for Managing Process Definition

Managing the process definition effort involves the full range of management issues. Although many of the points made elsewhere in this chapter have management components, the guidelines here directly address leaders of process definition efforts.

Process definition should be an example of a well-run effort.

1. Set explicit, realistic goals—both near and long term.

2. Adopt desired process behavior. While one cannot reasonably expect your software process definition effort to be much better organized and executed than your software projects, you should strive to adopt the next round of improvements desired of such projects. For example, if you expect software projects to use sound estimating procedures, the process improvement program should use them. If you are aiming toward having a defined software process, the process definition effort should define its process first.

3. Use the 11-step scale (Figure 4-7) to determine local cultural norms in handling risk or need to change (Grove 1983; Redwine and Riddle 1985; Sage 1993). Build a culture within the process definition effort (and hopefully the whole process improvement program) that is climbing the 11-step scale (Figure 4-7) ahead of the rest of the organization.

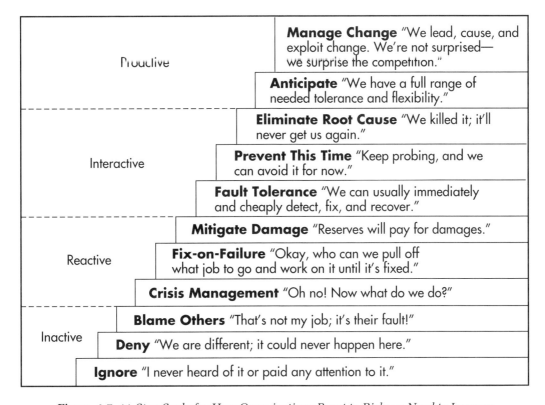

Figure 4-7 *11-Step Scale for How Organizations React to Risks or Need to Improve*

4. Explicitly manage uncertainty and risks. Be particularly sensitive to the need to provide your sponsors with near-team, tangible successes. Though process improvement economics is in its infancy, strive to justify process improvement efforts from the perspective of return on investment.

5. Have your own explicit process improvement effort.

Respond to your customers.

1. Listen to process users and sponsors (e.g., the steering committee). Follow the motivations, the threat or risk vectors, the money, the process users' needs and their customers' needs in deciding what to do. Motivated process definition users are the keys to success.

2. Be aware that the list of stakeholders may change. Try to obtain support broad enough to include likely new stakeholders (successors). This affects the amount of time and resources needed to get commitment.

3. Increase sponsor and management commitment and enthusiasm by building increasingly open, ongoing relationships with more key persons, and ensure that they see you as yielding solutions, not surprises.

4. Rotate process users through the process definition effort.

5. Have validated requirements for your process definition efforts.

6. Measure the size of your end-user base, relative success, and end-user satisfaction.

Integrate the process definition effort with organization processes.

1. As far as possible, involve yourself in all related planning (including budgeting) and with similar initiatives.

2. Increase awareness, coordination, and integration across software process improvement and definition efforts throughout the organization.

3. Ensure that the process definition effort's own processes integrate smoothly with other organizational processes.

4.3 USING METRICS TO STEER TOWARD SUCCESS

The purpose of metrics is to increase objectivity by providing a common measure with which to compare different phenomena or the same phenomenon at different times. In addition to the considerable benefit derived from using metrics, there is also the risk of mismeasurement or misinterpretation. This section covers important characteristics of using metrics to help you analyze, control, and predict your process improvement activities. Metrics are examined both from the perspective of benefits and from the perspective of associated risk.

4.3.1 Important Characteristics

There are many important aspects to metrics, but four are particularly important:

1. **Metrics must correlate to the phenomenon being measured.** From one perspective, metrics are intended to facilitate insight into some phenomenon in the real world. The intent of the metric is to change in some manner that is consistent with changes in the phenomenon being measured. If a metric does not correlate to what it should measure, it is useless. The more closely changes in the value of a measurement parallel change in the characteristics being measured, the greater is the usefulness of that metric.

2. **Metrics must measure something of interest.** In addition to correlations, metrics must also measure something that is interesting. Interesting is invariably subjective, but the concept is crucial nevertheless. It is too easy to define a large collection of metrics and spend disproportionate amounts of time and effort measuring characteristics that yield little, if any, valuable insight. From this perspective, *interesting metrics are those that provide you with insights that affect your decisions or your actions.* Clearly, when you find that you largely ignore a particular metric and it does not influence your thinking, that metric has ceased to be interesting for you.

3. **Metrics must reflect something that can be influenced.** Another key characteristic of metrics is that the measure relates to something that can be influenced. There is little value gained by measuring something that has no relation to anything that can be influenced. Curiosity may be satisfied, but if the metric monitors something completely outside your sphere of control and if nothing related to that metric can be influenced by you, the metric does not allow adjusting a process to achieve changes in the data reflected by the metric. If the metric can in no way provide you with any useful guidance on how to alter the phenomenon being measured or your actions with respect to that phenomenon, then the metric is essentially meaningless.

4. **Metrics must support making corrections or predictions.** One of the primary benefits to metrics is their use in validating predictions. For example, when proposing changes to a process model, attempt to predict what effect the changes will have on the metrics monitoring that process. When proposing a new or modified process, such proposals should be accompanied by claims to the effect that metric A will go up by x units and metric B will be reduced by about y percent. One value to such predictions is that they more precisely communicate the expected benefit from instituting a particular change.

Of even greater value is the fact that this approach can contribute to verifying whether the actual results of the new process match the predicted results. If results are generally as predicted, there can be a higher degree of confidence that the predicted benefits will be manifested. If changes in the metrics are running opposite to their predicted direction, it may be time to consider reinstituting the original process and reexamining the new process.

It is not always the case that when the predictions are wrong, the process is wrong. It could be that the metrics are not measuring what they seem to be measuring or that confounding influences are affecting the measurement and not being considered in the interpretation. Simply put, the problem may not be what is being examined but the way it is being examined. Fortunately, using metrics to make predictions is a self-correcting problem. Either the metrics are high quality and your ability to make predictions improves, or the metrics are not high quality and the lack of predictability causes you to reexamine and improve the metrics. In any event, you gain insight and make progress.

4.3.2 Incorporating Measurement in Process Definition

Considerations of what measures to include involve three factors: a minimum uniform set, measuring to meet your organization's goals, and a set of measures for each activity (and possibly each other type of item, e.g., artifact).

When establishing measures for an activity, a useful rule of thumb is to include measures of input size and quality, resource usage, and output size and quality. This generally implies size and quality measures for products that could benefit from standardization across activities.

4.3.3 Metric Support for Process Tracking and Cost Modeling

To implement process models, you need to accumulate software process and product information. Many existing accounting systems maintain costs in terms of activity-based models. Yours should do so in terms of the activities in your process definition.

Activity-based models use a bottom-up approach to software development cost estimation based on an analysis of the costs of the individual activities that comprise the software development process. Activity-based models are especially effective in an environment in which you have established a software experience database and use that database to feed back information about the process to improve the process.

The cost estimation methods usually base estimates on a function of the software product size. In turn, the development schedule is estimated as a function of the cost estimates. The size, cost, and schedule parameters are closely related.

If your software development organization is at process maturity Level 1, you probably have no experience data in a database. By the time your software development organization is at SEI process maturity Level 2, repeatable, you will have established a software experience database and accumulated sufficient data so that you can calculate unit costs for the main activities of software development (e.g., requirements definition, design, code and test, integration and test) and apply them on a project basis.

An activity-based model is built by assembling and ordering the activities that compose the development process to be used to produce the intended software product. The activities that form your development process may be from a previously used process, or they may come from a modified version of a previous process with some activities removed and other activities added. Alternatively, they may be a selected subset of activities from a menu of activities. An activity-based model enables you to begin by using the resource consumption (cost) for each of the activities in the development cycle, such as requirements analysis, preliminary and detailed design, code and unit test, computer software component integration test, and computer software configuration item system test. Your project may not use all of the repertoire of possible activities. For example, if you are developing a new version of an existing system, you might not have any preliminary design in your development process. Define your software development cycle in terms of known and measurable activities based on your organization's experience as contained in your experience database.

4.4 TRAINING-ORIENTED PROCESS REPRESENTATIONS

A key component of any process improvement program is process training. The challenge is to develop high-quality, cost-effective training courses. Due to the sometimes significantly diverse needs found in varying audiences, training material must also be flexible and adaptable. One of the most challenging types of courses to develop and deliver effectively are courses that strive to communicate the entire domain of process improvement. This type of course must deliberately balance sufficient generalization to ensure the entire domain is covered and sufficient detail to ensure that practical and essential concepts are conveyed.

During the first half of 1993, a CMM-based process improvement course was developed by the Software Productivity Consortium for delivery to consortium member companies (including Lockheed, Boeing, Martin Marietta, Grumman, Vitro, SYSCON, Rockwell, Aerojet, and similar aerospace and defense corporations). The course was initially taught to a diverse audience of member company personnel at the end of June 1993. Since then, the course has been taught on site at several member company locations.

This section gives a brief overview of the objectives, layout, and content of the process improvement course and then focuses on the lessons learned in the development and delivery of the course. Insights gained from creating and providing this course are discussed in combination with recommendations for how you can better evaluate, design, develop, and deliver process improvement—related education and training.[1]

4.4.1 Objectives for Process Improvement Education and Training

The stated objectives of the consortium's process improvement course were as follows:

- Educate participants in practical techniques on developing plans for, inserting, and managing process improvement.

- Introduce participants to methods for identifying areas for process improvement.

---

[1] This material is extracted from a paper developed by the author and presented at the Sixth Software Engineering Process Group National Meeting, Dallas, Texas, 1994.

- Introduce participants to the development of process improvement action plans.

- Educate participants on techniques for institutionalizing process improvement.

- Reinforce the participants' understanding of this material through the use of hands-on exercises.

- Provide an opportunity for participants to discuss and compare their experiences and understanding of process improvement.

The course used four break-out or lab sessions to help reinforce key concepts. It should be noted, however, that training participants in process improvement was not a goal for this two-day course. Instead, the primary objective was to provide a relatively balanced, full spectrum or worldview of process improvement.

4.4.2 Overview of the Process Improvement Course

For the purposes of the course, the overall objective of a process improvement program is to design, develop, and field "a flexible, well-understood set of processes that facilitate efficient and effective achievement of business goals." Consider the implications of these four key words:

- **Flexible:** Capable of being changed.

- **Well understood:** Comprehensible, documented, and trained.

- **Efficient:** Allows the business organization to be profitable or competitive.

- **Effective:** Delivers products the customer values.

Process improvement is often more difficult than originally anticipated precisely because "flexible" and "well understood" tend to be contradictory goals, as do "efficient" and "effective." Achieving a practical balance between these seemingly conflicting goals is critical to any successful program of process improvement, and how this balance can be achieved is a key part of the course.

The course is divided into five major sections, each with several supporting sections.

1. Identifying and Understanding (includes: Approaches to Process Improvement, Overview of the CMM, Targeting Areas for Process Improvement, and Organizational Barriers and Catalysts for Change).

2. Preparing and Planning (includes: Building an Infrastructure for Process Improvement, Action Planning Overview, and Risk Assessment).

3. Implementing and Managing (includes: How to "Work" a Process Improvement Plan; Institutionalizing Process Change; Process Representation, Definition, and Modeling; and Additional Techniques for Process Improvement).

4. Measuring and Monitoring (includes: Verification and Validation, Defect Detection and Reduction, and Metrics and Trend Measurement).

5. Continuous Process Improvement (includes: Strategic Implications of CMM Levels 4 and 5).

The course approaches process improvement with a CMM emphasis (Humphrey 1989) but also includes support concepts for a more general view of process quality (Harrington 1987) and software engineering practices (Radice and Phillips 1988).

4.4.3 Lessons Learned from Course Development

To develop this course, a call for slides was sent to the consortium technical staff requesting any electronic or hard-copy slides that people thought were related to process improvement. We hoped that a couple of hundred slides would be submitted. Nearly 2,700 slides (including hard copy) were received. Lesson learned: Anyone working on anything thinks he or she is working on process improvement. A first-cut pass at the slides yielded slightly over 600 that seemed directly usable. This was cut to 400 slides, which were then smoothed, augmented, integrated, and submitted to the reviewers. This was still too much material for a two-day course. The slide count was then reduced by nearly half, and reintegrated.

Following are several additional lessons learned during the development of this course.

Forget "agreement"; even achieving consensus will be difficult. There is no single right approach to process improvement. Depending on a person's background, perceptions, and understanding of process issues in general and local process issues in particular, what seems right can vary significantly. It is better to approach process improvement course material as a "feasible region." You can defer specifics until you arrive on site and have further information about the audience, their circumstances, needs, constraints, and similar other factors.

Extensively reference the material of others. Each passing month seems to yield considerable information on process improvement efforts conducted both nationally and internationally. It is not uncommon to see the same types of advice or findings surfacing simultaneously in unrelated efforts. Distill, cite, and include this material with your own. It is easier to get the resulting composite material past your reviewers if you don't have to defend every point personally. Additionally, by communicating a variety of insights, you provide a more robust and objective course for your attendees.

Collect material for a five-day course; then cut until it fits into two days. Far more material was collected for this course than was actually used. As a result, the course was repeatedly evaluated in terms of what could possibly be eliminated without losing key concepts. This approach can yield a course that wastes little time on incidental or superfluous issues.

Use short, modular topics. A process improvement course can be approached as a highly modularized field of study. At a minimum, it is easy to see that each key process area (KPA) in the CMM can be rendered into a standalone "plug-compatible" topic. The advantages to this approach are the opportunities to exclude or include modules as a function of specific audience needs and to rearrange topics to suit customer preferences. Using short, modular topics also simplifies the process for upgrading various modules. Low topic coupling improves the likelihood that module upgrades will not cause cascading changes in other material.

Cite sources inline. When slides present information that is derived from another source, cite that source (by name, not reference number) directly on the slide. This information helps everyone. Reviewers can immediately distinguish between material that is cited and claims made by the course developers. Inspectors can more easily identify and verify that cited material is true to the original. Class attendees have readily accessible pointers they can use if they desire additional or background information.

Citing sources also helps the instructor. At a minimum, it provides a visual reminder as to where the material originated. This gives the instructor the freedom, if desired, to give contrary examples without implying that the displayed material is wrong.

High-fidelity, meaningful labs are extremely difficult but essential. It can be very challenging to develop lab sessions for the attendees that are meaningful and have a high correlation to real-world issues. This is especially true if you need to limit your time in lab sessions. Based on experience, key process improvement issues that can be successfully conveyed during, for instance, a 1-hour lab are communication, team dynamics, organizational culture and dynamics, peer reviews, and process definition. Topics that need more lab time are risk management, measurement, and action planning.

Show it in pictures. Everybody says this. However, this is particularly important in a process improvement course. On-site presentation of material is much more effective when tailored to site-specific issues. It is very difficult to change substantially the way you talk to a slide when that slide is nothing but explicit text. It is quite easy to talk to a graphic in significantly different ways: changing emphasis or perspective or providing anecdotal support, for example, as circumstances require.

Do not trust the results of dry-run presentations. The problem with dry runs of a presentation is that there is often little correlation between the results of the dry run and the results of a real class. Although an unsuccessful dry run typically indicates the course (or instructor) is not ready, a successful dry run does not really mean that a course will be successful when presented to a (sometimes considerably) different audience. This inconsistency increases the importance of designing your process improvement course to be flexible, modular, and tailorable to various audiences.

Uncouple end-of-day topics. Again, the issue is one of audience. What do they know, what do they want, and how deeply do they want to examine various topics? Until you are in front of the class, it is very difficult to answer these questions. Therefore, design the course so that your end-of-day topics are virtually standalone. You want the opportunity to be able to break off a day of class at any of several different topics. You do not want to be in the position of ending class early because the next three topics should all be presented at that same time (thereby overloading the next day's schedule). Nor do you want to rush through those three topics, giving them superficial treatment.

Include contradictory material. Some material will be applicable to some circumstances, other material applicable to different circumstances. If the circumstances are sufficiently different, the supporting material can appear contradictory. It gives you considerably more flexibility to include material that contradicts information presented elsewhere in the course. When you do this, however, be sure you can either give examples to support how each of the approaches can be right given different circumstances, or take the position that you personally do not agree with one—or possibly both—positions.

4.4.4 Lessons Learned from Course Delivery

Developing a course can yield a variety of insights and lessons learned. However, there is nothing like spending a couple of days presenting your material in front of a real audience. Particularly in the area of process improvement—where unique circumstances are the rule, not the exception—each time you present the course you are likely to acquire a wealth of new information. Lessons learned from teaching the process improvement course fall into two general categories: (1) lessons relating to better ways to present the material or otherwise conduct the class, and (2) lessons relating to process improvement in general. The second category represents feedback from attendees about successes and problems they have encountered or heard about while trying to study, change, or otherwise improve processes.

4.4.4.1 Lessons Related to Conducting the Class

These lessons reflect course-related issues or insights that resulted from, or were reinforced by, conducting the process improvement course. Because audiences varied significantly, the following lessons learned reflect issues that are largely independent of audience type.

Include usable return-on-investment (ROI) case studies. From one perspective, it is regrettable that ROI is such an obstacle to initiating or continuing process improvement. There are clear and significant benefits to process improvement that do not easily convert to dollars (improved morale, better communication, less stress, increased motivation, reduced risk of litigation from defective products, etc.). Nevertheless, there is an element in many organizations that must have a clear ROI for any business initiative—and typically they have the power to prevent or eliminate funding for process improvement. Class attendees know this, and they invariably appreciate ROI case studies in the course material. This allows them to study and, if needed, present or use that information within their own organizations.

Deliberately keep some key issues off the slides. There are at least two good reasons for keeping material off the slides. First, it allows you recovery time in the event your course is running behind schedule. Second, attendees get very tired, very quickly, when slides are all you use. Having graphics-based concepts in your instructor presentation notes allows you to present and discuss material with the class that they perceive as "value added" (beyond the slide material). Flip-chart drawings are best; they allow you to tack or tape the various free-hand drawings around the classroom and thereafter easily reference or point back to them.

You cannot have too much material on lessons learned. Two sections of the consortium's process improvement course are composite lessons learned from various published sources. Although this material is in slide format, it was quickly discovered that there was a more effective way to communicate the information. During those sections, students are asked to work in small teams of three or four and annotate the slides with their own lessons learned. Each slide (or two) represents a different topic area, and students are asked to add at least one lesson learned to each topic. To ensure all topics receive attention, half the class is asked to start with the last topic area and work backward. After this mark-up session, each topic is revisited, and the students openly and informally discuss their annotations, opinions, experiences, and personal lessons learned. (The material presented in Section 4.4.4.2 was principally acquired in this manner.)

Include *at least* two labs per day. Break-out sessions, labs, group discussions, video, and other changes of format help maintain high attendee attention. Labs are particularly effective at making the material personal for the student. As a general rule, the more labs you work into your course, the better your students will understand and retain the material.

An early, first-day lab session is difficult; do it anyway. The problem with most labs is that they need to be preceded by a fair amount of lecture. Consequently, many courses have morning lectures and afternoon labs. It is typically more effective to intersperse lecture and labs, and it is especially useful to have an early lab on the first day of the course. This has two significant positive effects. First, students quickly realize they are not facing a full day of sleepy lecture. Second, the attendees start to become more cohesive—more of a team.

Do not conclude a day with a lab. An entire day of class (especially if it is the second or third day) is very tiring for the attendees. Additionally, if you are presenting the course on site, most attendees will be within walking distance of their desks—and an increasing backlog of work. These factors tempt attendees to skip an end-of-day lab session. Avoid an end-of-day lab if at all possible. (The assumption here is the lab is 90 minutes or less. Attendees are less likely to skip, for instance, an all-afternoon lab.)

Do not expect (or try) to teach the material the same way twice. This lesson again reflects the fact that process improvement audiences have widely varying needs, experiences, and circumstances, and they come from sometimes significantly different organizational cultures. Therefore, it is important to prepare instructor's notes for each offering of the course. It is equally important to ignore those notes if the audience or process improvement circumstances are not what you anticipated.

Overbook your classes. Process improvement is an area where people tend to think that other people need to know more. It is increasingly common for people to be told they should attend a course on process improvement. The problem is that not all of those being told to attend have the same level of interest. Further, it is politically incorrect (if not culturally impossible) for someone to state outright he or she is not interested in process improvement. Therefore, lack of interest tends to manifest in the form of a last-minute crisis or high-priority interruption that requires attention. They "plan" to attend your class; they just do not show up. Consider signing up 25 people if you want a class size around 20.

Highlight material that you do not agree with. You do not want to put yourself in the position of having to defend everything on every slide. This too easily leads to an adversarial relationship with the course attendees (or with your reviewers). They disagree with a point; you feel you have to defend it. It is highly useful to include material in the course that you do not agree with. Ideally, present some of this material early on the first day (even the first hour) of class. When you present it, state your opinion; then ask for theirs. This makes it more comfortable for students to share their experiences; they can agree with you, agree with the slide, or present some variation. In any event, you have explicitly demonstrated to the students that it is perfectly acceptable for them to take issue with any of the material and to share observations or counterpoints. The result is a much more participatory class, where you leverage not only your own experience and knowledge but also the experience and knowledge of everyone in the room. This considerably increases the value of the course for the attendees (and yourself).

Worst (but most likely) audience: veteran SEPG members. The consortium's process improvement course lasts two days. There are approximately 18 topics covered. Certainly, there are other topics that could be added. But even at 18, they must be covered in about 14 hours of actual contact time. Some topics are 30 minutes; a couple are 90 minutes. Regardless, the best that can be done is an overview of each area. Veteran SEPG members rarely need an overview, they need nuts-and-bolts details. Paradoxically, veteran SEPG members are the ones are most likely to be aware of your course offering and have the best chance of convincing management they need to attend.

Best (but least likely) audience: Novice practitioners and management. The best audience for a full-spectrum process improvement course is the unusual mix of novice practitioners and management. The former group appreciates the introduction and worldview perspective. The latter group typically wants insight into process improvement in general; they are not necessarily interested in (and do not have the time for) low-level mechanics.

Most frustrated population: Right-brained people. Attendees in process improvement classes have vastly different levels of enthusiasm and frustration. Generally, the most frustrated people are the "right-brained," sensitive, human-factors-oriented people. They can see their way to a better process but are amazed at how hard it is to work a cultural change in an organization. Analytically oriented people tend to accept small improvements more readily.

Leave space for one or two site-sponsored topics. Typically, there are some process areas with which the client is quite happy. For example, they may like their measurement program or their inspection process. Whenever possible, have them prepare and present that part of their process to the class. This gives the audience a much higher sense of involvement, concept ownership, and applicability.

Highest-interest topics. The top three highest interest topics in the process improvement course are (1) change management, (2) culture, and (3) measurement (amazingly enough). As presented in the consortium's course, these are all topics that extensively emphasize human factors.

Lowest-interest topics. The three topics that attendees seem least interested in are (1) organizational infrastructure, (2) alternative (non-CMM) approaches to process improvement, and (3) risk management. The low interest in organizational infrastructure appears to result from the fact that the attendees have very little influence over that. The lack of interest in non-CMM approaches seems largely pragmatic: with the course lasting only two days, there is barely time to present even a CMM-based perspective on process improvement. Finally, risk management does not seem to be what concerns people. They are reasonably confident that they can manage risk *once they are aware of it.* Risk *identification* is a high-interest area.

Emphasize human issues; deemphasize technical issues. There seems to be a growing consensus of opinion that there is nothing particularly challenging about the technical side of process improvement (people have successful assessments, they successfully develop action plans, etc.). The weak link in the chain is trying to get the users to change the way they work. This is where process improvement efforts fail. It appears the key challenge is in behavioral engineering, not software engineering.

Target the edge of the "cultural envelope." It is not so difficult for those involved in process improvement to see what the "right" process is for an organization. It is much more difficult to see the type and amount of change an organizational culture will tolerate at a particular moment in time. You can push the edge of the cultural envelope and still have a successful process improvement effort, but step beyond that edge and the culture will prevail every time. A critical aspect of having a successful process improvement class is evaluating the organizational culture of the attendees. This allows you to emphasize the types of change they may be able to work initially and to distinguish those from the types of change they should defer.

4.4.4.2 *Lessons Learned on Process Improvement*

Inevitably, an interactive process improvement course yields lessons learned from the attendees. These reflect the attendees' experience at the various companies they have worked for during their careers, experiences they have heard about from others, and insights they have gained from workshops, conferences, and other places. A few highlights are summarized in this section.

Primary (sole?) source of real-world failure: Implementation. Process improvement efforts are not prone to catastrophic self-destruction. Instead, if an effort fails, it is usually by slowly running out of momentum, support, and, consequently, funding. The critical hurdle is implementing the changes. Most cultures are generally quite willing to allow process engineers to assess, plan, document, and develop training courses. When it actually comes time to change the way people work, that is a different matter altogether.

Largest obstacle to initiating process improvement: Lack of a major crisis. It can be exceedingly difficult for an organization to initiate a program of change when that organization is successful at what it does. A major crisis is a great catalyst for change. Lack of a major crisis causes people, reasonably enough, to be resistant to change. In this type of environment, one of the strongest arguments you can use is crisis mitigation. That is, wouldn't be better to change in lieu of having to experience a crisis, as opposed to waiting until the crisis occurs, and *then* taking action?

Second largest obstacle: Legacy systems. When a company has been successfully doing work in a given area for 15 years, why should it change? If a legacy system or program is in its final phase, then its process probably should not be changed. However, if the company wants to prepare itself to work in different markets or to be more effective and efficient on the legacy program, then process improvement should be given serious consideration.

Third largest obstacle: Borderline "personal services" contracts. One of the arguments for process improvement is efficiency: doing more with less. Regrettably, if an organization is involved in personal services type of work (that is, the organization provides people to a client and is paid in direct proportion to the number of people provided), then the organization does not necessarily need to worry about efficiency. Arguably, that is the client's problem. Although it seems tactically advantageous for a company to tolerate an inefficient process under these circumstances, strategically it is risky. At some point, a competitor will likely get the attention and business of the client by claiming better efficiency.

Rite of passage: Wasting money on unused process definitions. There seem to be very few organizations that have not *tried* to document their process. However, as one person so aptly put it, "Let me tell you two things about your process documentation." (He was addressing a room full of people he did not know.) "First, it's covered with dust. Second, none of the pages are dog-eared." No one in the room argued. Writing process documentation is not difficult. Efficiently writing usable process documentation is the challenge.

Greatest unknown: Adjusting compensation to reward process improvement. It is no surprise that people do what they are paid to do. What is surprising is how many people forget that. Virtually all organizations pour additional money, talent, resources, and attention into crisis projects. The boringly competent project manager often goes unnoticed. An organization that consistently rewards people for crisis management will, appropriately enough, find itself constantly dealing with crises. The hard question is, How do you make process improvement an integral part of salary evaluations and bonus distributions?

Biggest SEPG mistake: Isolation from users. Successful process improvement is often characterized by high levels of ongoing interaction between the SEPG and the intended users of the new process(es). However, user involvement in process improvement is often difficult. First, the SEPG may be in a separate geographic location. In this case, email, review of draft process documentation, and surveys can be used to keep the users involved (and to gain valuable feedback). Second, and more difficult, the SEPG may not be allowed to "interfere" with or otherwise delay the engineers working on a tight (read, "crisis") project. Under those circumstances, the best option for the SEPG is to run away. Fast. Find a project that actually *wants* help.

Second biggest SEPG mistake: Giant steps. Something about working with software seems to make us think in on-off terms. Either there is no time or budget for any process improvement, or else everything has to change as fast as possible. Tempering enthusiasm about process improvement may seem counterproductive, but it is very important if you want to keep expectations in line with reality. It is far less risky to achieve a series of small, sure, positive changes than to attempt dramatic process convulsions.

Major challenge: SEPG scope of authority versus process improvement scope of use. When an SEPG develops new or improved processes, those processes are often intended for use in some subset of the organization. However, it can easily occur that not everyone in the subset recognizes the authority of SEPG. Even if they do, they still may not be willing participants of change. If there are any misalignments among SEPG scope of authority, SEPG product scope of use, and end-user (including management) interest in and support of the SEPG effort, there is proportionate risk of unsuccessful process improvement implementation. Regrettably, scope of authority versus scope of use is commonly not something the SEPG can control. These issues typically are inherited from—and, hence, need to be resolved at—the management level.

Forget "top down." Pursue "pockets of excellence." Many organizations pursue process improvement as an organizational change that must proceed from the top down. This can work if you have reliable commitment at all levels of management. However, if your organization is sufficiently large and contains a number of managers who are not yet convinced that process improvement should be pursued (or, more likely, they think the timing is wrong, the approach is wrong, or both), then the pursuit of establishing pockets of excellence is likely to be more successful.

Simply stated, you build a pocket of excellence by finding a set of projects that need change and then focusing on and working with those projects to carry them to the next degree of process improvement (which may or may not represent a change in CMM levels).

With the top-down approach, reluctant managers often take the position of "you're not forcing that stuff on me." With the bottom-up, pockets-of-excellence approach, those managers are a little more inclined to (eventually) take the position of "how come money is being spent to improve those other projects and none is being spent on my project(s)?" This is exactly the relationship an SEPG needs. Instead of being viewed as an unwanted intrusion, the SEPG is viewed as a source of help.

Layers of SEPGs require layers of steering committees. Many organizations are too large or too geographically diverse to have a single (and effective) SEPG. Consequently, it is not uncommon to encounter the concept of regional SEPGs, and a national SEPG within these organizations. There may even be two or more local SEPGs within a region. Generally, if you have layers of SEPGs, it is best to have corresponding layers of steering committees. The issue is one of relative clout. A regional SEPG may have only nominal influence on a national steering committee. However, if a regional SEPG can sway the regional steering committee, they can then rely on the regional steering committee to champion their cause(s) at the national level.

Biggest negative surprise: Metric-induced behavioral changes. As a rule, people do not like to be measured. If they are measured, they invariably "work the measure" so that it shows them in a favorable light. Consequently, when introducing or changing a metrics program, you might inadvertently cause people to manifest unintended behaviors. This occurs for the simple reason that they know you are measuring them, they know what are considered "good" measurements, and they adjust their behavior accordingly—even if it is counterproductive.

Consider the following example. You announce to the engineers on a project that you will be measuring, during the peer review process, how many defects they find and how long they take to find them. You tell them the objective is to find ways to improve the inspection process so that more defects can be found in less time. As the data start coming in, some engineers appear to be "better" at defect detection; they find more per unit time than other engineers. This makes other engineers uncomfortable, they too want to be better. They've also noticed that during inspection preparation, a lot of defects are found quickly. These are, of course, the obvious problems, and can be detected at the rate of, say, 30 an hour. However, obscure or subtle defects are much harder to find, and an engineer might notice their detection rate of obscure defects is, for example, 2 an hour. So, what will our metrics encourage the engineer to do? Find the obvious errors and then stop. This will yield an impressively high defect detection rate. Clearly this was not the goal.

Any metric program should be approached cautiously, and the process (and people) being measured must be carefully monitored for unexpected and undesirable side effects.

Moving from Level 2 to 3 is much easier than moving from Level 1 to 2. It seems paradoxical at first, but there is accumulating consensus that it is easier to go from Level 2 to Level 3 than it is to get to Level 2 in the first place. A considerable source of an organization's culture is its management. Consequently, trying to change the way managers work is, essentially, trying to change the culture of an organization. The Level 2 KPAs primarily focus on management-related issues. Hence, achieving Level 2 in many organizations amounts to a cultural change. Level 3 principally focuses on the engineer. Engineers are often much more ready and willing to change than their managers, partly because managers became managers because they were successful at doing things—the way they used to be done. It is also because line management often has multiple priorities. That is, they are told to support process improvement but hold to schedule and reduce costs. If a manager is paid to get product out the door on schedule, then that clearly communicates how the manager needs to arrange their priorities. There is growing evidence that once management is comfortable with and supportive of process improvement, the rest of the organization is quite willing to participate.

Most difficult question: "How do we change our culture?" Many of the lessons learned have centered around the importance and difficulty of organizational cultural change. In a process improvement course, the attendees become aware of this and want to know how to change their culture. Since each organization's culture is unique, the answer to this question must be correspondingly unique. However, there are some principles that you should point out to the attendees. First, the culture of an organization is carried within the people: no people, no culture. Hence, you cannot change a culture directly; you must try to influence people. Second, there appear to be at least two mechanisms that have demonstrated the capacity to influence reliably how people behave within an organization: (1) change the way you compensate, reward, or otherwise positively reinforce them and (2) change what, when, where, and why you collect measures.

4.4.5 Representations for Training: Conclusions

One of the primary lessons learned from preparing and delivering process improvement training courses is that it is easy for people involved in process improvement to do things backward. That is, the traditional approach is to design and define a new process or methodology and, when it is complete, put together a course to teach it. However, due to the excellent feedback typically provided during courses on process improvement, you are encouraged to consider the advantages of creating and presenting the course much earlier in the process development and delivery cycle. Paradoxically, a course on an improved process (or a course on process improvement in general) should precede, not succeed, the detailed development of that process technology. Only *after* a set of techniques and supporting material demonstrates value (ideally, to a variety of audiences) can we legitimately begin to claim that we have validated that approach to process improvement.

It has long been acknowledged within academia that one of the best ways to understand a topic is to try teaching it to others. Development and delivery of courses related to process improvement can be — and should be — an integral part of your process development process.

4.5 TOP-DOWN VERSUS BOTTOM-UP ORGANIZATIONAL PROCESS DEFINITION

We have looked at the key factors affecting the success of process improvement initiatives within organizations: the importance of organizational change management, technology transfer, metrics, and training. This section examines the advantages and disadvantages of top-down versus bottom-up process definition and modeling.

4.5.1 Organization Abstraction Levels

Organizational process definitions are intended to convey both constraints and flexibility. You want to constrain the processes in such a way that you can pursue organizational goals while avoiding disasters, yet you also want to preserve—and pass through to program and project managers—the flexibility they need to select how to engineer end products efficiently and effectively. This allows you to vary a process to different circumstances even though the final product is essentially the same.

Consider the housing industry. One process for building a house is to hire an architect, design a custom house, and have it built to your exact preferences. A different approach is to go to a developer who might have a hundred or so predesigned types or styles of houses—some intended for cities, some for mountains, others for coastal communities. As a buyer, the process allows you to select from some reusable designs and tailor the design to suit your preferences. Tailoring options may be extensive, such as whether you want the optional garage, porch, or three-story model. The result of each of these processes is the same: you have a house that you expect to suit your needs. Similarly, you might also visit a builder who is constructing a townhouse community. In that scenario, you may have the option to select from six or seven basic models. For each model, your tailoring options could include whether you want a fireplace, upgraded carpet or appliances, or a bay window for the living room. Here too you end up with the same product: a house to live in. But the process that produces and markets these houses is markedly different in each of the examples.

Independent of these three process variations for building and marketing houses, there are certain invariants that hold true for each of the processes. For example, there are electrical codes, building codes, standards for plumbing, structural stresses or load maximums, federal and state zoning, and tax requirements. These are, effectively, "organizational" process constraints that must be adhered to independent of the type of process being used.

As this example shows, process definitions can—and should—occur at different levels of abstraction. The number of abstraction levels appropriate is a function of the size of the organization and its type. However, as shown in Figure 4-8, one way to analyze levels is to think about process definitions at five levels of abstraction:

1. Organizational process definitions.

2. Business area process definitions.

3. Program process definitions.

4. Project process definitions.

5. Project plans.

Note that these options span the entire spectrum from the highest or least detailed level (organizational definitions) to the lowest or most detailed level (a workable plan that is used to enact and track the process). Consequently, when commencing a long-term process improvement effort, one of the first questions to answer is, "Where should we start?" Section 4.5.2 presents a top-down view of process definition that may be appropriate for organizations with stong funding, support, resources, and time available for the process definition effort. Section 4.5.3 presents a brief discussion on how to develop organizational process definitions via pockets of excellence. This is likely a more appropriate approach for organizations facing time, budget, resource, or other constraints on their process improvement effort.

4.5.2 Top-Down Software Process Definition

The software industry is beginning to recognize the importance of standard and defined development processes to producing consistently high-quality software within budget and on schedule. However, unique project characteristics may affect a project's ability to perform to a previously defined development process; that is, different process drivers generally result in software development processes that may vary slightly to significantly from project to project.

Many process groups today are faced with the difficult task of defining the product development process for a large, complex, and highly variable organization, as well as for the multiple and diverse projects within that organization. Finding the right set of solutions requires structure and discipline, including careful analysis of the problem, designing an architectural framework within which the problem can be decomposed (a top-down perspective) into smaller, more manageable pieces.

Similarly, imagine trying to build a large, complex software system without first designing a software architecture: interface problems are prevalent, requirements are implemented

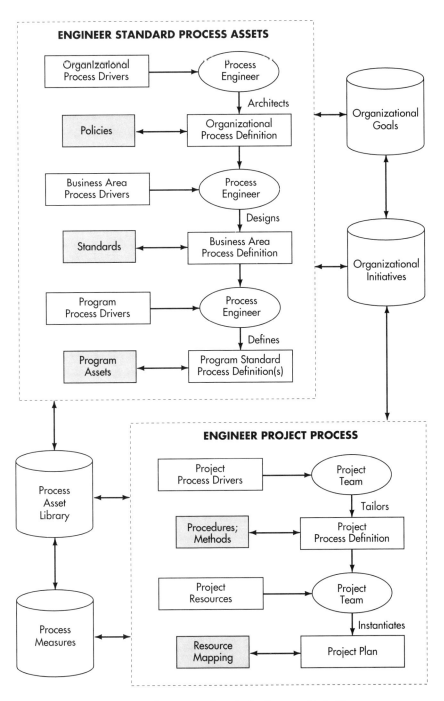

Figure 4-8. *Abstraction Levels for Process Definitions*

inconsistently or not at all, and design constraints are violated. Like software engineering, one approach to process engineering is to represent complex interactions among process steps through a high-level process architecture that can be subsequently refined and elaborated. That is, process engineering can follow an approach that elaborates the process through different forms of representation and level of detail until an enactable, or performable, level is reached with appropriate reuse and tailoring at each level.

Many software organizations have expended a significant amount of time and resources to produce voluminous process descriptions. Often these descriptions do not correspond to the processes actually performed during software development or maintenance. Some key problems may cause the disconnect between how a project actually performs to produce its required product and the organization's standard process model, including the following:

- Organizational process models developed at too high a level of detail.

- Organizational process models defined at too low a level of detail.

- Organizational process models that mandate inappropriate life-cycle model(s).

To a large extent, these key problems are symptoms of the difficulties encountered when attempting to tailor an organizational process definition for a specific project. To resolve tailoring problems, it may help to consider the process model in terms of reusable assets:

- Organizational process definition

- Business area process definition

- Program process definition(s)

- Project process definitions

- Project plans

- Process asset library

- Process measures database

- Policies

- Standards

- Program assets

- Procedures and methodologies

- Resource mappings

Figure 4-8 shows activities to produce and continually evolve the appropriate process assets to the appropriate level of detail. In addition, it specifically surfaces the impact of process drivers that place requirements on each level of abstraction or elaboration (Software Productivity Consortium 1994).

At the organizational level, top-down process engineering can start by identifying existing process assets, including activity specifications, method descriptions, standards, and artifact definitions, and using them as the basis for creating an organizational process definition. Parts of the process definition may be unique to a given business area. Where no appropriate material exists, you may need to create it from scratch.

An organization may be divided into two or more business areas—coherent markets characterized by customers possessing similar needs. In this case, you may find it useful to detail one or more standard process definitions based on the unique drivers of the appropriate business areas.

Additionally, within a business area two or more major programs may be occurring. Typically each program will have requirements in common with all the other programs (and hence, can be considered business area drivers) and each program will have requirements unique to it. These are the program process drivers.

Project process definition addresses product-specific characteristics, such as the product risks and life cycle and is based on the process definition developed for a specific program, business area, or organization (if the concepts of business areas and/or programs do not apply). The information identified in the program process definition is fully elaborated in the project process definition, which is turned into an enactable process plan by mapping people and other resources available for the project, establishing budgets and schedules, and other components.

Sections 4.5.2.1 and 4.5.2.2 discuss each of these top-down process engineering life-cycle activities in terms of the key process assets that result from each and the process drivers that place requirements on the development of assets.

4.5.2.1 Engineer Standard Process Assets

As shown in the top box of Figure 4-8, higher abstraction levels of process definition have the goal of producing standard process assets. This includes creating organizational definitions, business area definitions, and program process definitions.

Organizational process definition involves defining organizational context and organizational process policies. You analyze and document how organizational procedures are enacted currently and resolve conflicting interpretations of these procedures to obtain a consistent view of organizational policy. To synthesize this information at an organizational level of elaboration, the process is typically represented by a set of organizational policies, with appropriate cross-references to show policy relationships.

Organizational process definitions vary from one organization to the next, based on unique process drivers. Process drivers that may place requirements on the identification and definition of process policy at an organizational level include:

- Investments (such as hardware, software environments, training, etc.)
- International standards
- Infrastructure and culture
- Government rules and regulations (such as federal acquisition regulations)
- Market trends
- Performance goals

If an organization is not further divided into business areas, then you should develop an integrated set of program process definitions.

The phase define business area process definition(s) involves decomposing organizational policy and augmenting that process information with additional detail. Typically, business areas are subject to several internal and external standards, especially product standards. At this level, the process definition will need to communicate, at a minimum, the organizational policies and standards that drive one or more of the programs conducted within the business area.

To develop business area process definitions accurately, you must first determine what constitutes an organization, business area, or other area. Instead of an entire company, an organization can also be a division or a functional area within the division. One company may feel that it has several divisions, each with sufficiently different missions, customers, products, and cultures to warrant creating several business area-specific process definitions. Another company may determine that one process definition is sufficient because only one type of business is pursued.

If the business areas have specific operational environments that are significantly different, then multiple business area process definitions can be developed based on each area's unique process drivers, such as:

- Technology and business strategies
- Product lines
- Methods particular to the business area
- Risks specific to the business area
- Industry standards for the business area
- Existing product assets for the business area, such as development environments and reusable software

You can define specific business areas at a lower level of granularity than at the organizational level because of visibility into product lines of various programs within the business area. This visibility allows you to determine, select, or identify applicable process and product standards.

At the program level, you can identify the type of products produced within the program, and hence, the life-cycle models for key products in the product line. You then begin to elaborate the life-cycle models with partially ordered steps or activities that will help guide projects in achieving each of the key product's life-cycle states. Thus, this phase is known as **define program process definition(s)**.

The process definition at the program level will facilitate construction, evolution, and product reuse by identifying and defining standard process steps at a summary level. The goal is to identify the partially ordered key process activities, which compose the overall process, and elaborate the primary relationships between them. The resulting definition is still at a high level of abstraction and typically has the following characteristics:

- Partially ordered sequence of process activities
- Key process activities defined in terms of their functions, primary inputs, and major outputs
- Naming conventions and standards
- Standard process templates or formats
- Interface specifications
- Composition, selection, and tailoring rules

Again, at the program level, the process definition typically does not decompose the key process activities in any great detail. You generally represent it graphically and support it by text or templates that define the high-level scope, objectives, and function of each key activity and the policies and standards that guide, cause measurement of, or constrain those activities.

4.5.2.2 Engineer Project Process

The result of the above types of process definition is a repository—typically called a *process asset repository*—of reusable process assets. These assets are used to facilitate the development of project process definitions, which are tailored to the needs and circumstances of individual projects and can be instantiated and enacted.

Project process definition is a two-phase activity that yields a preliminary and final project process definition. In the first phase, you work with the process manager to select the process asset(s) that will be used on the project to guide the key product's development phases. This preliminary project process definition is a description of a project's process and includes a selected life-cycle model. It identifies the various options for process steps, the options for performing them, their various connections to each other, and alternative mappings to the product life-cycle phases. The preliminary project process definition is developed based on specific product drivers, such as:

- Product-specific requirements
- Product-specific development standards
- Product-specific methods
- Product-specific risks, such as performance or integration problems

This phase can be relatively uncomplicated if an organization is subdivided into business areas and programs, and the program has defined its product line and the life-cycle models that best support each key product. If this is the case, there may be several preliminary process definitions "on the rack" for a project to choose from, thereby eliminating the need to custom-build the preliminary project process definition.

During the second phase of this activity, you use the preliminary project process definition to derive a final project definition. During this phase, you and the project manager elaborate the preliminary project process definition by selecting from among the alternatives presented in the preliminary project process definition. This is the time to tailor the final project process definition specifically to the project situation. Generally, the final project process definition is developed by selecting and tailoring the process step specifications that will meet the objectives of each product life-cycle stage, identifying the work products that will be produced by each step, and choosing the methods that will be used by each step. The final project process definition is tailored based on project specific drivers, such as:

- Selected product life cycle
- Project objectives, such as producing zero-defect software
- Project constraints, such as customer requirements or environment
- Project risks or potential problem areas, such as limited access to users

The project manager can define the project process definition either before it is performed by the project team or in parts, as long as each part is defined prior to performance. In either case, the result should be a (progressively more) final project process definition that represents the road map that the project team will follow to reach each life-cycle state.

In the **instantiate process plan phase**, the project manager instantiates the final project process definition by using it as a template for the project schedule. The manager also uses the process step specifications as templates for specific project tasks, assigns specific agents to each task, and estimates the time and effort needed to complete the tasks. Specifically, the project manager instantiates the final project process definition by assigning schedule and resources to produce an enactable process for the project team to follow. The project manager makes these allocations depending on such drivers as staff availability and experience, contract milestones, contract budget, and risk mitigation.

The result of instantiating the project process definition is a project plan. The project plan should document, or provide a reference to, everything that is needed to enact the project process. The process plan specifies the resources necessary for enacting the process, the relationships of these resources to process steps, the products produced by these steps, and any constraints on enactment or resources. Resources include human process agents, computer resources, time, and budgets. Relationships refer to the estimation or assignment of resources to process steps to meet project objectives (Feiler and Humphrey 1992).

Again, the final project process definition does not need to be instantiated completely at one time; often it is better to define and instantiate it in increments based on lessons learned and an increasing knowledge about project and product process drivers and awareness of changes in the circumstances surrounding the project as the project evolves.

To put the **enact project process** into practice, the project manager performs resource leveling in order to validate that the proper resources have been allocated to each task, and initiates, monitors, and controls the execution of each task according to the project schedule. An enactable process consists of a process definition, required process inputs, assigned enactment agents and resources, an initial enactment state, an initiation agent, and continuation and termination capabilities. An enacting process may be in a suspended state if an assigned process agent is not available or other process constraints are not satisfied (Feiler and Humphrey 1992). The project team enacts the project process by following the plan and performing their assigned tasks.

4.5.3 The Pockets of Excellence Approach

Section 4.5.2 described process definition in a top-down manner. There are, of course, countless other approaches. A substantially different approach is to build pockets of excellence within the organization by defining the process from the bottom up. Once you have backed into your organizational process definition, you can then reverse course to improve and optimize the process definitions in a top-down manner. Then, after reaching and improving project-level definitions, reverse course again and start working your way back up through the abstraction layers. Highlights of the bottom-up approach are presented in Sections 4.5.3.1 through 4.5.3.10.

4.5.3.1 Identify High-Value, Low-Risk Process Kernel

Typically, as a result of either a formal or informal process assessment, you will have identified several areas of a process that are candidates for improvement. This provides an opportunity to create a pocket of excellence within those projects that were assessed. An important decision is which process problem you will address first. For example, do you want to improve the configuration management process, the quality assurance process, project tracking, project management, or peer reviews? Each of these process areas, when defined, yields a process kernel that becomes part of the process asset library.

When you are selecting which process kernel(s) to define, keep the following advice in mind:

- Prefer smaller process areas to larger.

- Prefer simpler process areas to those that are more complex.

- Prefer a process that is almost adequate, as opposed to one that is totally inadequate.

- Prefer a scope of effort that is shorter as opposed to longer.

- Prefer a process area that the projects consider unthreatening.

To summarize, when you start defining your process, first select a process kernel that allows you to show a quality process definition in a short amount of time that has a high likelihood of being accepted and used on the projects. As you gain in experience and ability, you can extend your effort to define more difficult or challenging process areas.

4.5.3.2 Identify Projects for Pocket of Excellence

Once you have identified the process kernel you want to define, identify the initial audience you expect to use the intended process definition. Generally the audience will consist of one or more projects included in the original process evaluation or assessment. It can certainly be the case that another project, not included in the original assessment, may be a good candidate for the newly defined process. However, to whatever degree that audience feels it is "different" from those assessed, you likely will find it correspondingly more difficult to convince them the newly defined process is applicable to their circumstances. Regardless of how similar you think projects are, the managers of each of those projects will almost invariably consider their project unique.

Try to find projects with audiences truly interested in incorporating the newly defined process. As incentive, remind them that their advice will be unobtrusively solicited throughout the process definition effort. Keep in mind that you are not necessarily defining a new process for them to use; the goal of this particular phase may well be simply to define the process as it is currently being performed.

4.5.3.3 *Interactively Define Common Process Kernel for Target Projects*

It is almost imperative that you involve end users in the work of defining their process. Involvement includes, at a minimum, conducting interviews, even if they are quite brief, on how they do their work and how they think it should be done. Have the end users (at their discretion, but try and encourage participation) review and comment on various draft releases of the process definition. Later, continue to involve users by maintaining an open door policy for ongoing feedback after a version of the process definition has been baselined and officially released for use. Also, visit them to determine their perceptions about and use of the process kernel definition.

4.5.3.4 *Pilot Instantiation of Process Kernel on Selected Project*

As you develop the definition of the selected process kernel, you will perceive different degrees of interest and support from among the projects involved in becoming a pocket of excellence. It is generally the case (but certainly not always) that the project that offers you the most support or shows the most interest is also an ideal candidate for piloting the newly defined process. The purpose of the pilot is to acquire that last degree of insight based on feedback from real-world application.

To whatever degree possible, try to pilot the newly defined process kernel on a project that:

- Is being managed by someone who is interested in piloting the newly defined process.

- Is staffed by people who are interested in piloting the newly defined process.

- Is not under unusual time constraints.

- Is not under unusual budget constraints.

- Is not already involved in significant change.

- If a complex process kernel, has successfully piloted prior newly defined processes.

In practice, however, the overriding factor that drives success is whether you can find a project where the people want to participate in piloting the newly defined process.

4.5.3.5 Build Valid Process Definition

Piloting the newly defined process will invariably yield insights into the applicability, usability, and intrinsic value of your process definition. Use the pilot as a means for continuing to improve the overall quality and value of the process definition. Do not make substantial changes to the process definition without validating the impact and value of those efforts on your pilot project. If the project completes before you are done with the process definition or if the project must, for whatever reason, disengage itself from the pilot effort, be sure to find another pilot project. It is extremely important that you validate your process definition before releasing it to your general audience.

4.5.3.6 Transfer Validated Process Kernel to Other Projects in Pocket of Excellence

Once you have a defined process kernel validated, your next step is to export that definition for use on other projects targeted for the pocket of excellence. Do not just ship out guidebooks. For each project you have targeted, attempt to arrange with the project manager for a roll-out meeting of the new definition. This can be as short as 10 minutes if you defined a process the project was already trying to follow. For duration, we highly recommend the roll-out meeting not exceed 30 minutes. The roll-out is **not** intended to train people on the process. It is only intended to make the project aware of:

- Who you are.
- What you are doing.
- Why you are doing it.
- How it is intended to help them.
- How they are expected to use what you are providing them.
- How they can reach you if they have questions, comments, concerns, or recommendations.

After the roll-out meeting, you will need to follow up and support the project aggressively—and possibly help the project manager arrange for training. Ideally, you will find that the project accepts, absorbs, and appreciates having the process definition available. However, when they find using the process definition to be awkward, excessively time-consuming, or confusing, you will certainly want to be aware of that and take steps to address these issues at the earliest opportunity.

4.5.3.7 Select Next Process Kernel

Generally, unless you have a high degree of expertise, we discourage you from attempting to define several process areas simultaneously. This is especially true if one or more of the process areas are complex or involve areas of possible contention regarding best approach. You should first secure two or three solid—and sequential—victories.

When you are reasonably certain that your first process definition has high quality and will be of value to the projects, you can begin work on the next process area. The process proceeds in much the same way as already described, with the exception that in time you will have the expertise to address confidently two or more process areas as part of a single process definition effort.

4.5.3.8 Select Next Pocket of Excellence

Once several process areas have been defined and transferred into the projects within a particular pocket of excellence, look for other areas within your program or business area that can benefit from the existing set of process kernels. For each new pocket of excellence, select a project to pilot the newly defined process kernels. You need to verify that the new pocket of excellence is similar enough to the original one. If the similarity is sufficient, projects in the new pocket of excellence will very likely perceive the process definition(s) to be applicable to their situation, valuable, and usable. If the definitions are not accepted by the projects, it may be that the new projects have process problems in different areas or the new projects are too different.

4.5.3.9 Distill Process Kernel Definition(s) for Multiple Pockets of Excellence

At a certain point, as you continue to export defined processes to more projects, you will find that there is a need to address new problems that did not surface during your original assessment. Certainly this may indicate that it is a good time for another assessment. However, it is also true that you do not need to wait for an assessment before you define a process. All that is necessary is for the organization to acknowledge that process problems can at least partially be addressed by developing or improving upon the definition of one or more process areas and then authorizing that work.

This work proceeds as described in Section 4.5.3 (selecting one or more process areas, interactively defining them with the involvement of a subset of your intended audience, piloting/validating, etc.). This work leads to continuing extension and expansion of your process asset library.

4.5.3.10 Abstract Up to Organization-Wide Process Policies

Projects will resist a given process definition if they consider the definition to be inapplicable given local project circumstances and characteristics. In other words, the defined process is not sufficiently tailorable to that project's needs.

This becomes the catalyst for you to evolve your process definitions to progressively higher (less detailed, more flexible) levels of abstraction. Note that as a general rule, you distill higher levels of abstraction by throwing details away, not by adding more details. The level of detail and the number of necessary constraints are less at the program level than they are at the project level. Similarly, the level of detail and the number of necessary constraints you need at the business area level are less than what you need at the program level.

You can start at the bottom, or most detailed level, and define your organizational process as follows:

- Take your project plan. Throw away the names of people, dates of work, and similar enactment information, and you have a good foundation for your project-level process definition.

- Take your project definition. Throw away information that is specific or unique to that particular project, and you have a good foundation for program-level process definition.

- Remove program-specific information and life-cycle models, and you will likely be left with two major types of information: standards with which the process must comply and organizational policy. Jointly, these serve as a good foundation for business area process definition.

- If you eliminate standards that are relevant only within, but not between, business areas, then the remaining information—typically policy intensive—can be an excellent foundation for an organization-level defined process.

The five levels of abstraction used in this material may not be applicable to your organization. You may, in fact, be quite comfortable defining your processes at two levels: organization and project. Nevertheless, the key point remains the same: at every level of abstraction, strive to define only what **has** to be defined. Keep your process definitions as spartan as possible, and strive to preserve maximum flexibility at every level of abstraction. This permits your project managers and engineers the greatest opportunity to leverage their experience, expertise, and talent for addressing unexpected problems and for capitalizing on unforeseen or unusual opportunities.

4.6 SUMMARY

This chapter covered key organizational issues and considerations when performing process improvement and presented variations among process definition and modeling situations with the objective of providing guidance for improving your own process improvement and process definition efforts. Much of the guidance derives from seeing what others have done in the past—particularly what they have overlooked. However, you can certainly be successful without following every piece of advice, and this guidance should always be evaluated with respect to each situation.

Each time you want to improve your process, consider process definition as an ongoing function with a permanent set of organizational issues, considerations, constraints, processes, and relationships. Initially, some of this may be a luxury in your situation, but you should revisit these aspects as you are considering your second or ongoing effort.

As a word of caution, when process improvement efforts fail, it is often due to either organizational, cultural, or management reasons rather than technical ones or by taking on too much too soon, rather than taking an incremental approach, building incremental experience, and providing incremental benefit. The road to successful process improvement is the one road that leads to success in other projects: plan, manage, do quality work, be efficient, involve users, get early results, demonstrate ongoing success to sponsors, and, as your competence increases, progressively and incrementally expand the breadth and depth of your effort.

Eventually, expanded breadth and depth starts introducing another problem: rapidly increasing amounts of process knowledge, information, and data that need to be efficiently managed. The next chapter returns to the details of process representation; it provides a comprehensive examination of the vast quantity and types of process-specific information that organizations might consider collecting and guidance on how you identify what is important to your organization.

Chapter
5

PROCESS TEMPLATES

5.1 COMPREHENSIVE MANAGEMENT OF PROCESS INFORMATION

Capturing, modeling, and managing all important information about the processes performed within an organization can potentially become a huge, labor-intensive, and expensive effort. Information management tools can be extensively leveraged not only to reduce work load, but also to help ensure integrity, completeness, and consistency of process information. While Chapter 4 examined the broad issues and human factors relating to the success of process improvement efforts, this one refocuses on a critical and often forgotten point: all successful efforts at process improvement rest on a foundation of numerous process representations used to support process analysis, design, development, and implementation. These representations are information intensive; failure to manage this information efficiently and effectively commonly leads to failure of your entire process improvement initiative. Therefore, this chapter returns again to the issue of process information management and presents an extensive discussion of hundreds of different types of process details and how those details can be linked or related to other types of details, how and when they can be used, why you might need to, or not need to, collect and track various details, and so forth.

The breadth of this discussion notwithstanding, remember that your first priority must be to ensure that all process information you collect has value to your organization. As a word of warning, you can be certain that you do *not* need to collect or use *all* the details (referred to as "fields" on templates) discussed in this chapter. However, different organizational goals and circumstances render greater or lesser value to different process details. As you review the following, determine what subset of information is necessary to achieve your goals, given your circumstances. Additionally, remember that relative value always remains a function of objectives and circumstances; if either change, you will need to re-examine the value of the process information you're maintaining and the value of that which you are ignoring.

How do you know what process information has sufficient value that it qualifies as important to your organization? If an item is important you will be able to answer, or get answers to, all of the following questions:

- Where can this information be obtained?

- Who needs it?

- Why do they need it?

- When will they use it?

- How will they use it?

- What benefit is achieved through its usage?

The following discussion of process information uses the concept of process templates and fields of information to provide a context for you to consider process information management, especially with respect to how automated tools might best be leveraged to support your process definition efforts. Although the discussion generally uses the perspective of information inheritance and relationships, this does not preclude using, for example, an object-oriented approach for capturing and maintaining process information.

5.2 FRAMEWORK FOR PROCESS TEMPLATES

To define a software process adequately, your definition must extend beyond the activities that make up the process. You must define the types of products produced by the process; the resources required; and the key relationships among products, resources, and activities. To determine what a template-based model should capture, you need to analyze the concept of a process. Figures 5-1 through 5-4 briefly review prior material and provide the motivation for the conceptual model used as the foundation for determining what information you may need to capture about your process.

At the simplest or most abstract level, a process uses externally provided inputs to produce externally available outputs (Figure 5-1). Figure 5-2 shows two classes of inputs: variable and fixed. Variable inputs are transformed in some manner to produce the output; they are called *products*. Examples of fixed inputs are machines, meeting rooms, management staff, engineering staff, and administrative staff. Fixed inputs are referred to as *process resources*.

It is diagrammatically advantageous to separate products from process resources because they play different roles in the process representation. In Figure 5-3, resources are at the bottom of the circle representing the process. The revised diagram implies that input products are directly related to the output products, but the performance of the process depends on the *process resources*. At this point, the model represents a process as an activity that converts input products to output products by relying on a set of process resources. The model must

Figure 5-1. *Process Model: Level 1*

Figure 5-2. *Process Model: Level 2*

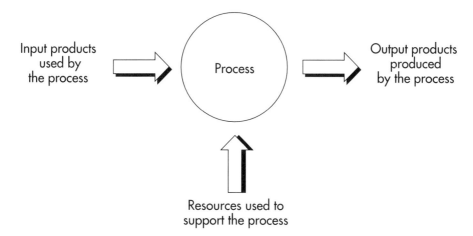

Figure 5-3. *Process Model: Level 3*

also show, as indicated in Figure 5-4, that a process is a set of activities subject to control. Examples of process controls are quality standards or constraints on available resources.

The definition of a process is now as follows: a **controlled** set of **activities** that uses **input products** to produce **output products** by relying on a set of **process resources**.

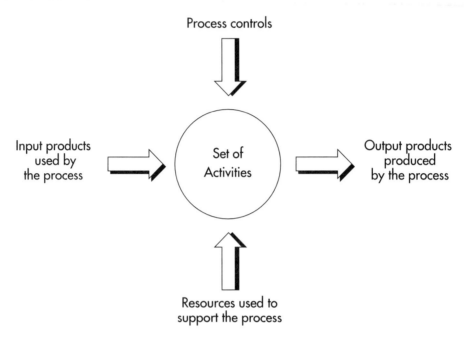

Figure 5-4. *Process Model for the Template-Based Approach*

If you are familiar with the IDEF or SADT methods for process modeling, you will note that this perspective is analogous to the approach used in those representations. Consequently, IPDM provides a way of incrementally collecting material that you can use to create these and other graphic models.

The model shown in Figure 5-5 directly corresponds to the templates discussed in detail in this chapter:

- **Activity templates**, which capture information about the activities occurring within a process. They define the entrance criteria, exit criteria, and key relationships for those activities.

- **Product templates**, which capture information about the inputs and outputs of a process.

- **Support templates**, which capture information about people and mechanisms needed to support a process. Only the people aspect, or roles, are discussed here.

Eventually you will need to model risks associated with the process. Risk can take a variety of forms—for example, risks related to the input products, different risks related to resources, and still other risks related to various activities (Figure 5-6). In short, the potential for and existence of risk surrounds all aspects of process.

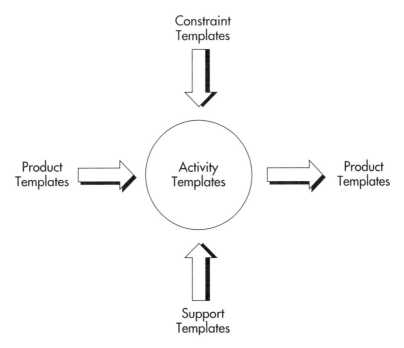

Figure 5-5. *Meta-Class Templates*

5.2.1 IPDM Conceptual Model Summary

To summarize, the conceptual model of IPDM is simple. A process is a set of activities that typically:

- Has inputs.

- Produces outputs.

- Requires resources.

- Is subject to constraints.

- Potentially embodies risk (see Figure 5-6).

   IPDM also assumes that multiple activities will be underway simultaneously and that activities, products, and roles can sometimes be described in terms of their state. State information is "knowable" by any activity. This convention simplifies modeling because an activity does not have to produce an output describing its state for subsequent reference by other activities.

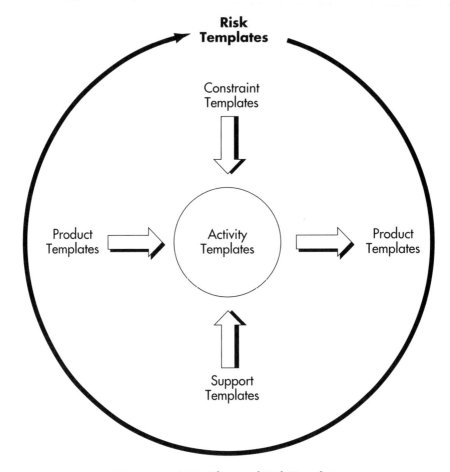

Figure 5-6. *Meta-Class and Risk Templates*

You can build process models that include previously defined models. For example, if a process requires use of certain configuration management procedures, the process model can incorporate a configuration management process model "by reference" on one of the templates. In this way, process descriptions that have been proved effective elsewhere in an organization can be reused when defining a project's process.

The templates and the associated graphical notation provide a simple means for capturing, manipulating, organizing, and analyzing process information. The graphical notation is used to provide a high-level view of the process and to show relationships between process information detailed on the templates. The process definition is contained solely in the templates; the graphical notation is used only to provide alternative views of the information contained in the templates. If you are using IDEF or another such notation, you can use the graphical notation of these methods in conjunction with the templates.

IPDM allows you to construct process models by a variety of process modeling methods. For example, if your process model is built using an object-oriented modeling technique, the product templates and states of products will play a key role in influencing the sequence in which activities occur. If you select this approach, you will not be describing the sequence of activities in terms of product flow but will instead describe product evolution in terms of sequenced activities. Conversely, if you prefer to use an activity decomposition technique, activity templates and the hierarchical and behavioral relationships that exist between them will be the primary tools in defining the process.

IPDM is not biased toward any particular process description paradigm. Object-oriented process models, functionally oriented process models, management-intensive process models, risk-driven process models, spiral process models, and others can be depicted using these templates. The primary differences will exist in the templates selected for use, the details allocated to these various templates, and the types of relationships established between the templates.

5.3 GOAL-BASED PROCESS DEFINITION

Before you perform process representation, you must first determine your goals and objectives and examine the constraints your current circumstances place on the achievement of those objectives. The objective of performing process representation is generally considered to be:

- To disseminate and train the process.
- To analyze and improve the process.
- To plan and control the process.

Similarly, you need to acknowledge and work within the limits of your organizational circumstances. As shown in Figure 5-7, organizational circumstances are ranked along a spectrum that ranges from having to be completely reactive to your current situation to being quite proactive.

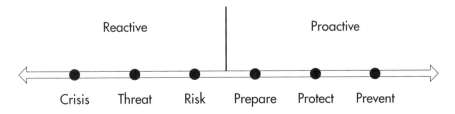

Figure 5-7. Organizational Circumstances

To review briefly, organizational circumstances consist of the following:

- **Crisis.** Typically, a crisis demands that your process improvement work must give the highest priority to reacting to the immediate situation and that no effort should be spent on anything not directly beneficial with regard to resolving the current crisis.

- **Threat.** A crisis is imminent. You can exceed doing the bare minimum necessary, but only if there are clear and near-immediate advantages in doing so.

- **Risk.** You can begin to pursue your process improvement objectives in a manner that begins to offer strategic advantages.

- **Prepare.** Your situation allows you to perform value-added work that better positions the organization for the next crisis. You have more time for analysis and redesign, versus process capture and documentation.

- **Protect.** Process improvement work is explicitly intended to yield processes that are sufficiently robust that they can withstand a variety of adverse impacts from circumstances outside the process (or outside of your ability to control).

- **Prevent.** Your circumstances allow for you to pursue the maximum degree of proactive process improvement. High-fidelity process models allow you to gain detailed insights into the impact of alternative and sometimes radical process redesigns. The objective is to prevent crises from occurring.

Having identified your process improvement objectives and your organizational circumstances, you are positioned to determine the process information you need to capture and manage during this iteration, or cycle, of process improvement.

5.4 IPDM TEMPLATE INFORMATION INHERITANCE

IPDM templates embody an information inheritance architecture that allows you to tailor or extend this methodology to suit your particular needs and preferences. However, before augmenting this methodology—and to understand the organization of material presented in Section 5.5—you need to know the inheritance principles

As described in this book, templates have four levels of information inheritance:

1. **Foundation template.** All templates are derived from a common foundation template.

2. **Meta-Class template.** Meta-class templates inherit common fields from the foundation template.

3. **Class template.** Class templates are derived from meta-class templates and add information unique to that template.

4. **Subclass template.** Subclass templates are used to refine and distinguish process information.

These four levels of information inheritance translate into two types of usage:

1. **Final template.** These templates are used for collecting data. In Figure 5-8, final templates are shown with a solid border.

2. **Contributing template.** These templates only contribute fields to final templates and are not actually filled out. In Figure 5-8, contributing templates are shown with a dashed border.

The foundation and meta-class templates are useful for discussing fields common to groups of templates and to facilitate tailoring the templates to site-specific objectives. This structure allows for easier construction and discussion of the templates and their fields. Furthermore, this approach facilitates the use of automated tools for designing, maintaining, and using electronic versions of the templates.

All templates have fields such as the following in common: Name, Unique Identifier, Description, Comments, and Revision History. Any field intended to be used on all final templates, regardless of type, is shown on the foundation template. The discussion of such globally common fields is found in Section 5.5.1, which describes the foundation template. All meta-class templates "inherit" these common fields from the foundation template. Each meta-class template adds information common to class templates of that meta-class and not common to class templates of a different meta-class. For example, under the activities meta-class, there are class templates for production and audit activities. These two classes have certain fields in common with each other, for example, entry criteria and exit criteria. Each class therefore provides space for a description of these criteria. Because of this principle of inheritance, any field shown at the meta-class level of a template appears on the class templates subordinate to that meta-class. All fields that the meta-class template inherited from the foundation template will also be included.

These are generalized templates, and it is expected—indeed, encouraged—that you will tailor them to the needs and characteristics of the corporate or organizational environment in which they are employed. Similarly, you can tailor these templates for the actual process notation favored by a given environment. The purpose of the hierarchical architecture in the template design is to facilitate the tailoring process.

The technique for tailoring is simple. Consider the scope of any new field you want to add:

- Will the new field be used on all of the final templates? If so, put the new field on the foundation template; all other templates will then inherit this field.

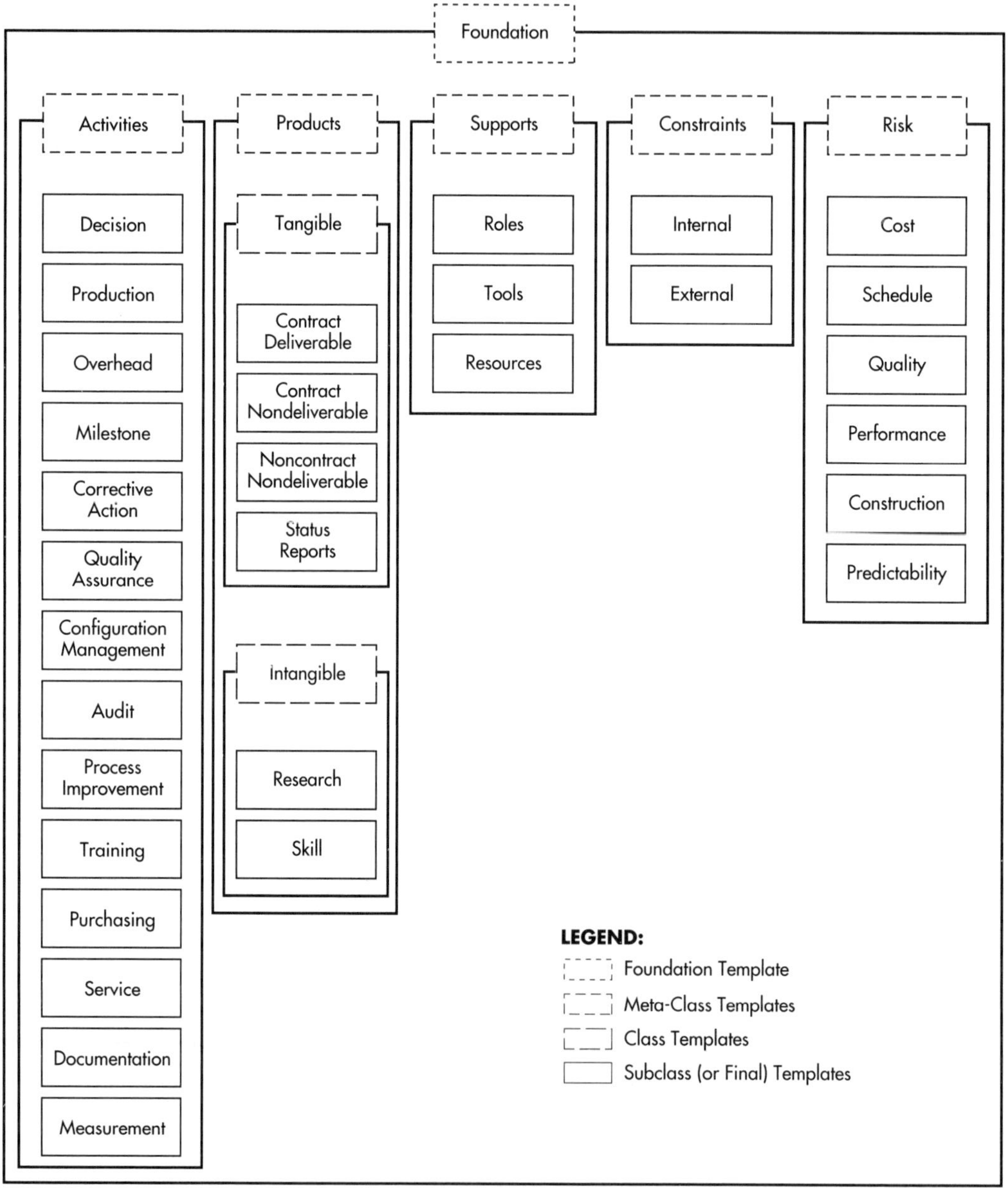

Figure 5-8. *Template Inheritance Model*

- Will the new field be used on both the role and the resource templates? If so, change the support template at the meta-class level and allow the role and resource templates, and any other defined support templates, to inherit it as a common field.

This approach makes it easy to introduce and document changes to the templates yet preserves the underlying consistency between templates.

5.5 IPDM TEMPLATES

As a general guideline, when you build a list of fields that you think are important, annotate each item with one of the following confidence values:

- Definitely Important

- Probably Important

- Possibly Important

Next, draft an architecture or schema of only those fields that are definitely important but ensure that the schema can be easily modified to accommodate data tagged as probably important (in the event it someday becomes clear such data are actually definitely important). Time permitting, investigate further into the possibly important data items and try either to upgrade their importance or remove them from your list.

Once again, heed this warning: your process templates and representations must be as lean as you can make them. Organizations have built highly successful databases that manage hundreds of process assets (different activities, products, etc.) but consist of only a couple of dozen fields existing in only a handful of files or tables. *Simplicity is of paramount importance.*

The remaining material in this section demonstrates the rich abundance of process details that you *can* track and gives explanations that better enable you to decide what you *should* track.

5.5.1 Foundation Template

Sections 5.5.1.1 through 5.5.1.3 present the fields on the foundation template. The type of information you need to collect is clustered into three different types of usage:

- Information used for process modeling

- Information used for generating model-derived process end products

- Information used for management and review of the process definition and modeling effort

5.5.1.1 Model-Specific Fields

Typically the first type of information you will collect is process information that applies directly to the process model itself. Of the fields described in Section 5.5, only a few are required for defining your process, the remainder are optional as a function of your goals. As you read the field descriptions, make a preliminary list of the fields that seem important to you. Keep in mind these two key considerations:

- The end products you want to produce

- The resources (time, budget, etc.) that you realistically expect to be available for this effort

Unique ID field. Each template requires a unique identifier. It is highly recommended that you adopt the following conventions:

- **Keep the identifier as short as possible.** Identifiers will be one of the most repeatedly used fields on the templates. Shorter names reduce the amount of typing or writing required when referencing templates by their identifiers.

- **Make the identifier meaningful.** It greatly facilitates understanding if you use abbreviations to build the unique identifiers. Probably the least meaningful identifiers are those that are constructed entirely of numbers.

Name field. This field is for the name of the template. Again, brief and meaningful names are best. In this field, there is no real advantage in prepending the names of ancestor templates. Indeed, doing so has the disadvantage of creating names that are too long.

Comments field. This field is for notes about the information on the template; it is not intended for information about the process being modeled. It is quite useful, when constructing and maintaining templates, to have a place where you can make notes to yourself or to other developers about things to be done, current problems, suggestions for changes, and so forth. This field is intended for that usage. Think of it as a "scratch-pad" area.

Depth field. This field represents the generation depth of the template. For example, in a hierarchical organization of activity templates, the activity template at the top of the hierarchy has a depth of 0, the first level under that template (or its "children") has a depth of 1, any "next-generation" child templates under Level 1 have a depth of 2, and so on. This information facilitates orientation while quickly scanning hard-copy printouts of templates. Using an automated tool, this field can be easily calculated by the tool, and hence would not require user input.

Purpose field. This field is used to provide a very brief explanation of why this process object is necessary. The motivation for having the process object (activity, role, product, etc.) is provided in this field.

Description fields. There are four types of description fields, and each has a specific use:

1. **Graphic Description.** The Graphic Description field provides a place to include a picture of the object being represented by the template. For instance, if the process object is the Inspection activity, then you might want to include a picture that graphically depicts the various stages of the Inspection activity and how those stages relate to each other. Slides, such as might be used in presentations or training, should be considered "graphics" even though a slide might just contain a list of bullets.

2. **Brief Description.** The Brief Description field contains a one-sentence (ideally, one-line) description of the process object. This field will be used repeatedly throughout end products whenever there is the risk that showing just the name of a process object may fail to inform the reader sufficiently.

3. **Overview Description.** The Overview Description field contains a detailed description of the process object in terms of its content, scope, and other characteristics.

4. **Summary Description.** The Summary Description field contains details about the process object. To understand how to use these two fields (Overview and Summary) properly think about exporting this information into a variety of outputs, such as guidebooks or proposals. Some descriptive information you want to print before you print the progressively more detailed information found on any child templates beneath the current template. It is also common to want to print some summary information (hence, the field name) after you have printed the child template details.

Generally use the Overview Description field to provide an overview of what you are about to tell them and the Summary field to provide a summary of what you just told them. Detailed material, from one or more generations of child templates, fills the void between. If a template has no children (i.e., it is a "final" template) there is no need to split descriptive information between Overview and Summary, as the information will be output contiguously regardless. In such circumstances, just use the Overview field.

Parent Template(s) (Multiple Occurrence). This field is a multiple occurrence field that contains the Unique IDs of the parents of the current template. In the majority of cases, any given child template will have only one parent template, but multiple parents may occasionally be useful in some areas of your process model. For instance, if you have a process object that describes how you conduct peer reviews, you may want to show it as a child under many different parent development activities.

Child Templates (Group of Fields). This is a multiple occurrence group of fields. Each information group is composed of four fields. For each child, you need to know:

- **Unique Identifier** (*multiple occurrence*). The identifier uniquely associated with the particular child of interest. Since there are typically two or more children, there will be a corresponding number of unique identifiers. Fields related to that child (type, tailoring, and proximity) will be grouped with each identifier.

- **Child Type.** Contains one of two values: the child is either a composition child or a specialization child. A set of two or more composition children is used to indicate that the parent is composed of each of the children, in union. Put differently, each child is literally a part of the parent, and the parent is a composite of all of the children. Conversely, a set of two or more specialization children indicates that the child templates are each a special form of the parent, and, depending on circumstances, just one of the children is selected. For example, consider a process model where one of the nodes is intended to represent a compiler for a programming language. The specialized children of that template may be a template representing an Ada compiler, another template representing a C compiler, and another for a FORTRAN compiler. The specialized child relation tells us that just one of these compilers is selected.

  Contrast this with a node that represents an inspection team. This template might have composition child templates such as Moderator, Scribe, Inspector, and Reader. In this example, the parent is composed of all the children (the team is composed of all the team members).

  From the logical perspective, composition children are an "and" relation to the parent (the parent is made of child-1 *and* child-2 *and* child-n), whereas specialization children are an "or" relation to the parent (the parent is an instance of child-1 *or* child-2 *or* child-n).

- **Child Tailoring.** The Child Tailoring field contains information about which children are required, which are optional, and so forth. These tailoring options allow for plans to be built from the process model, but which are tailored to the circumstances and process drivers of particular projects. The values for this field are:

  - **Required.** The parent requires this particular child, so there is no option to tailor it out.
  - **Recommended.** The child is typically included in the parent (in the case of a composition child type) or is one of the most common forms of the parent (in the case of a specialization child type). However, there is a waiver procedure available whereby a justification for excluding or not selecting that child can be evaluated and possibly approved.

— **Suggested.** It is within the authority of those planning or managing the project to use their own judgment to determine whether that particular child is included or selected. Generally, suggested children do become part of project plans unless there is a compelling reason to exclude them. In any event, they may be excluded at discretion and without going through a waiver process.

— **Optional.** The particular child is not typically included in project plans, but the person or persons planning or managing the project should be aware that an option to use the child exists; they may, at their own discretion, elect to choose or include that child.

— **Restricted.** Exactly the opposite of Recommended. If you want to include this child as part of your project plan, you will have to go through a waiver process that exempts you from the policy restricting the selection of this child.

— **Prohibited.** The child is not to be included (if it is a composition child) or selected (if it is a specialization child). No waivers exist. Although it seems unusual to define prohibited process objects, the concept becomes important as process assets become more abundant and tailorable. For example, as a function of different process drivers, an activity that is recommended in one life-cycle model may be prohibited under a different model. A process object would never be prohibited under all circumstances.

• **Child Proximity**. Contains one of two values: **local** or **remote**. Local proximity indicates that the information about that child is stored locally and, hence, is immediately available. Remote proximity indicates that although further information about the child is available, it is found elsewhere (such as in a completely separate database) and, hence, is not immediately accessible. The premise is that another template or set of templates exists elsewhere which further elaborates the nature and content of the child.

Transitions (Group of Fields). This group of two fields contains information about process objects that fundamentally change to different objects within a given model. The two fields in this group are:

• **Changed From/Unique ID.** Indicates the unique identifier of the template that represents what the object used to be.

• **Changes To/Unique ID.** Contains the unique identifier of the template that contains information about what this process object will eventually become.

These types of metamorphoses are quite rare within process models. Usually they occur only when products later become constraints. For example, a design activity might create, as an output product, a detailed design document. However during coding, it is typically more accurate to show the detailed design document as a constraint and not as a product. Note that if template A indicates it changes to template B, then template B must correspondingly indicate that it changed from template A. Typically, this type of bidirectional integrity can be automatically enforced in a database environment.

Additional Information (Group of Fields). This is a multiple occurrence group of fields that contain information about where additional material about this process object can be found. This includes the source material from which the information on the template was derived. These fields may also contain information about where someone should look for additional details (which may or may not also be available in other parts of the process model). This group is composed of the following fields:

- **Title** (*multiple occurrence*). Contains the name of the reference document.

- **Section** (*multiple occurrence*). Contains further information to facilitate easily finding any relevant information. Section is a repeating field under title (that is, for a given title, there may be multiple sections that have relevant information), and Pages is a repeating field under Section.

- **Pages** (*multiple occurrence*). Intended to carry a range of pages and would be used as a repeating field only if, for a given section, the reference information was in two or more groups of pages (e.g., Section-N pages 12–14, pages 21–25, page 36, and pages 41–51).

5.5.1.2 End-Product Fields

All the fields described in Section 5.5.1.1 are directly useful for modeling your process. However, you also need to capture information that makes the model information more usable in various end products. The fields in Section 5.5.1.2 contain information specific to creating usable process end products from the model-specific information.

Used Within (Group of Fields). This is a multiple occurrence group of fields that contain information about where the template information is being used or will be used and whether it can be used on the next build of that product. Specifically, this group of fields is composed of:

- **Output Object Name** (*multiple occurrence*). The name of the intended output artifact or product: guidebook names, the names of training courses, proposal names, and so forth. Special care must be taken that the same output product is always referred to by the same name. That is, the name must always be treated as a unique identifier.

- **Output Object Type.** Indicates the type of object within which the information will be used. (guidebooks, training courses, proposals, technical reports, operations manuals, project process manuals, etc.). For the purposes of automation, the information for this field should be provided by the environment as a function of the Output Object Name. That is, to ensure consistency, it is recommended that you construct a file of output objects that contains both their name and their type.

- **Include In Next Build**. A field with three options: Yes, No, and Unknown. During the development of process models and parallel development of process-related guidebooks and other materials, it is recommended that you repeatedly print incremental drafts to verify the scope, integrity, and quality of your work. This field allows you to indicate when you think a template has sufficient information and is sufficiently accurate to start being included in builds of output products.

Transition Text (Group of Fields). This is a multiple occurrence group of fields with material that facilitates the presentation of process information in the various end products. This group of fields consists of:

- **Output Object Name** (*multiple occurrence*). Identical to and used in the same way as explained for the Used Within group of fields. As a rule, it is illogical to have transition text for an end product that this template is not "used within." Consequently, the Output Object Name in this group of fields must match one of the Output Object Name fields in the Used Within group of fields. However, it is perfectly acceptable, even common, to have output objects listed under Used Within but for which there is no transition text.

- **Leading Transition Graphic.** Available for optionally storing a graphical image that depicts important information relative to the process object. As with all other references to graphics, this term is used to include any form or presentation of information that is targeted for output that is potentially graphical in nature—for instance, slide presentations—even though such presentations may consist of numerous slides that contain only text.

- **Leading Transition Text.** Contains textual information intended to improve the understandability or usability of the end product (but, again, this is information you do not need in the process model itself). Leading transition text is extracted before any other fields (such as the descriptive information) are taken from the template.

- **Trailing Transition Text.** Contains textual information intended to improve the understandability or usability of the end product (but, again, this is information you do not need in the process model itself). The trailing transition text is extracted after any other fields (such as the descriptive information) are taken from the template.

- **Trailing Transition Graphic.** Has the same purpose as the Leading Transition Graphic field but is used when you want the graphic to be presented after all the other transition and process information on the template.

Think of the mechanics behind the goal of automatically generating end products from the process model. You need to navigate the model algorithmically and extract information so that the information is output in the sequence necessary for the intended end product. Regardless of how powerful and intelligent the search and selection algorithms are, when you actually read the output—guidebook or training material, for instance—you will likely find places where the transitions between topics are awkward, jarring, or confusing. To improve the readability of that end product, it may be necessary to add some transitional text to smooth the flow of topics or information or provide content information useful to the reader or user of that product. To accommodate this need, go to the template whose information is presented in that part of the end product and add the necessary transitional material. That is, if you need a picture or some text (or both) before the process information on that template, use the leading transition fields; if you need a picture or text after the process information, use the trailing transition fields.

The purpose of these transition fields is to capture information that is important only with regard to the specific end product. For example, you may want to include a foreword at the front of a particular guidebook. Where do you put such information? This is information that is not part of the process per se but is still useful to have when building a guidebook derived from the process model. If you need to include such information, use transition fields to capture it.

Because transition material is entirely end product specific, on any given template you may have as many groups of transition fields as you do end products.

In principle, you can write an entire guidebook, proposal, set of training material, or other materials using nothing but the transition fields. You can get all the text to appear exactly in the order you want it and every chart, graph, table, and picture to be placed within that text at exactly the locations needed. However, in practice, you want to achieve this goal by *minimizing,* not maximizing, your use of the transition fields. Think of the transition fields as a form of insurance. The goal is to build a process model, populate it with information, and extract that information in ways that create completed materials. To some degree, you will improve those products by improving the structure and content of the model from which they are derived. However, at a certain point you will find that the model is fine and the information in it is adequate; the problem is with the characteristics, use, and requirements of the specific end product. This is the time to turn your attention toward using the transition group of fields.

5.5.1.3 *Management-Specific Fields*

The last type of information you need to consider collecting is information related to managing, reviewing, and ensuring quality as the work of process definition proceeds. The following fields are intended specifically for information that helps perform process definition efficiently and effectively. As a subtle distinction, it is not meant to imply this information is only of use to managers. The fields are useful in managing the effort. Paradoxically, the use of these fields reduces the burden on management personnel to watch the process definition effort closely because this information directly facilitates "self-management" by those performing the process definition work. Of course, this also provides management the means to evaluate progress achieved to date easily and quickly.

Requirements Traceability (Group of Fields). Arguably, this group of information, could be considered process model information, but, from a different perspective, the fact that a process model needs to depict a process that complies with some set of requirements (such as ISO-9000, or requirements derived from the CMM, etc.) is typically something that management elects to impose on the process. This group consists of the following fields:

- **Requirements Document Title** (*multiple occurrence*). Used for the name of the requirements document, policy document, standard, or something else that requires this particular process object. As with titles of other external documents, be careful to treat this field as a unique identifier. No two external documents should have exactly the same name, and an external document should always be referred to by just one name.

- **Requirement Unique ID.** Should be taken from the original source document or material. This unique identifier allows easy traceability between the process model and one or more requirements documents or standards. In some cases, it is useful to add extensions to the original requirements identifier. For instance, if the source document has requirement *x* that is explained over five pages, then you may find it helpful to make traceability references to: requirement *x*, paragraph 5, or requirement *x*, paragraphs 11 through 15.

- **Level of Satisfaction.** Contains one of the following values to indicate to what degree that particular requirement is satisfied by this particular process object: Very Low, Low, Moderate, High, Very High, Unknown. A single template might show that it satisfies one requirement to a moderate degree, another requirement to a very high degree, and a third requirement to a low degree. Additionally, a number of templates may be involved in satisfying a particular requirement, and though individually each template's satisfaction of the total requirement may be only moderate, taken together they might offer complete coverage and hence, as a collection, yield a very high degree of satisfaction. Consequently, a parent template can show very high satisfaction even though none of its children showed more than moderate satisfaction of the same requirement. Unless you have a means for quantitatively analyzing level of satisfaction, you may want to use an even simpler scale. A scale of Low, Medium, High, and Unknown will likely suffice in many circumstances. Regardless of the scale you select, always include the option Unknown, and use it as the default field value.

Assigned To (Group of Fields). This multiple occurrence group of fields is used to name the person or persons who are responsible for the template. This group is composed of two fields:

- **Name/Unique Identifier** (*multiple occurrence*)

- **Group/Unique Identifier**

As with other name or title fields, these names are considered to be unique identifiers and should be treated accordingly. Both fields may contain the unique identifiers of role templates. In that case, only the Name field should be directly input; the Group identifier would be found in the Parent field of the role template. In the relatively rare case of multiple parents, the Group field must match one of the parents. In lieu of using explicit identifiers, just type in this information.

Work Status (Group of Fields). This group of fields facilitates planning, allocating, and tracking the work involved in developing the process model and its ability to generate finished (or semifinished) end products. The fields are:

- **Percent Complete.** Used to carry a value between 0 and 100, where 0 indicates that essentially no work has yet been done on the template and 100 indicates that the work on this template is complete. If on some future date there is a decision to make major extensions in the details of the model, one of the first steps would be to downgrade the Percent Complete field to reflect how complete the templates are with respect to the new objectives.

- **Planned Information Capture Start Date.** Reflects the starting time of the effort in which, according to the plan, the content of the template will be entered. This effort includes time involved in research and conducting interviews to collect information.

- **Planned Information Capture Completion Date.** Reflects the completion time of the effort in which, according to the plan, the content of the template will be entered. This effort includes time involved in research and conducting interviews to collect information. The completion date is intended to reflect that period in time when the template is expected to contain a sufficient amount of information to be usable within the process model in general, one or more end products that are to be generated by the model, or both (depending on the goals of the current effort).

- **Actual Information Capture Start Date**. Reflects when work really was started.

- **Actual Information Capture Completion Date**. Reflects when work was completed. Again, the beginning of any major effort to update the templates (or a subset thereof) would include resetting all the actual capture dates back to null values in preparation for the next wave of work.

- **Template Development Status**. Used to indicate to management and others participating in, or interested in the progress of, the process definition effort. Each template is given a current status from the following list:
  - **Awaiting Development**. Although the template exists, no one has yet begun to work on it. Two aspects of development status can be inferred from another field. If the Assigned To field is empty, the template is not only awaiting development; it is also awaiting assignment to someone or to a group of people. If that field is not empty, the template has resources assigned to work on it, but that person or group has not yet begun the work.
  - **Under Development**. Work has begun and is underway.
  - **Work Temporarily Suspended**. Although work was started, it is currently in a state of suspension (so do not look for anything new until the status changes).
  - **Finished Incomplete**. Although more information could be added to this template, no further additions are expected at this time. This might occur when time or funding for an effort is running out, and work is being redirected to concentrate on high-benefit parts of the model.
  - **Finished Complete**. Work on this template is finished, and the content is sufficiently complete for the current usage.
  - **Finished to External**. Work is complete, and valuable information is available (typically in hard-copy form) that is not part of the process model. If this is the status of a template, there must be at least one entry under the Additional Information Available In field to tell the user where to look for the external information.

Version Number. For configuration management purposes, each template needs a version number in addition to its unique identifier. It is highly recommended that you include the date a version is completed as part of the version numbering scheme. This greatly facilitates reviewing prior versions of a template as a function of when the work or updates were performed.

Revision History (Group of Fields). Revision history provides information about the evolution of a template and the information it contains. This group of fields includes:

- **Revision Date** (*multiple occurrence*). Contains the date that a particular revision was completed. Consider this to be similar to a release date for the template. It is highly recommended that this not be the date the work is completed but the date when the template successfully passes your quality review process.

- **Resulting Version Number.** The new version number assigned to the template after updates have been made, reviewed, and approved. The most recent Resulting Version Number should match the Version Number field.

- **Update Comments.** Allows the person or persons who updated the template to provide brief comments on the nature of update, why the update was done, and similar other material.

- **Revised By** (*multiple occurrence*). Contains the name of the person or persons who created a particular revision. For any single instance of a revision date and resulting version number, there may be two or more people who participated in that revision. Be careful to treat this field as unique keys; that is, always refer to the same person by using exactly the same spelling.

Template Review Status. IPDM presumes a regular review process as part of building and maintaining your process asset library. This field and the following group of fields are intended to support the review process. There are five values for this field:

- **Review Needed.** The default value. Generally, whenever a template is created or whenever work begins on updating or modifying the content of a template, the template review status is set to Review Needed.

- **Ready for Review.** The person or persons working on the template consider it to be sufficiently complete and accurate to be reviewed. This does not necessarily imply that they have stopped working on or updating the template.

- **Reserved for Review.** The template is now "owned" by the review process. At this point, no further changes can be made to the template until it is released by the review group (i.e., until this field has been set to Review Completed). In an automated environment, the template should be locked, or permissions changed, to prevent inadvertent updates.

- **Under Review.** The template is moving through the review process. As with Reserved for Review, the template continues to be owned by the review process, and hence no updates, alterations, or changes are allowed.

- **Review Completed.** Those involved in the review process are ready to release the template back to the developers (or to those responsible for configuration management). Review Completed implies nothing about the results of the review. That information is conveyed in the Review History group of fields.

Review History (Group of Fields). Review History fields are used to collect information about the occurrence and results of reviews. This group includes the following fields:

- **Review ID** (*multiple occurrence*). Contains a unique identifier that allows you to distinguish one review effort from another.

- **Review Date.** Contains the date in which the review was completed.

- **Version Reviewed.** Indicates the version number of the template under review. A single version number may be subject to more than one planned review, such as a preliminary review and a final review, and may also be subject to one or more unplanned reviews, as would occur if the template failed to pass the review process.

- **Review Composite Result.** Contains one of the following values:
  - **Passed**. The template passed the review process without any moderate or severe issues being identified by the reviewers. If any trivial issues are identified, these are passed back to the developers so that they may update the template accordingly, but no further review is needed. If this review cycle is part of a baseline evaluation, then once passed, the template would be baselined before being released back to the developer(s).
  - **Passed Marginally**. One or more nontrivial issues should be addressed by the developers. These are suggested areas to be addressed; it is up to the developers whether they perform the rework. Regardless of whether the developers elect to address the issues, no further reviews are required to pass this phase of work.
  - **Passed Conditionally**. One or more nontrivial issues must be addressed by the developers before the reviewers will pass the template. Once the required rework is done, there is no need for a follow-up review. This does not imply that rework is not verified by, for instance, an inspection moderator but only that another review by the entire review team is not anticipated or expected.
  - **Failed Marginally**. If the reviewers decide that rework needs to be done, and due to scope or other factors the reworked template needs another review, they classify the template as either Failed Marginally or Failed Significantly.
  - **Failed Significantly**. In the reviewer's opinions, the template was not ready to be reviewed and needs substantial work before another review is requested.

- **Reviewed By** (*multiple occurrence*). A multiple occurrence field that contains the names of everyone participating as a reviewer. Each name is treated as a unique identifier.

- **Individual Review Result.** Indicates how each reviewer evaluated the product. For example, if five people reviewed a product, three of them might choose to recommend it be Passed Conditionally, while the other two might choose to recommend it be Failed Marginally. In such cases, either consensus opinion or policy would determine the review composite result. This field allows for distinguishing reviewer results prior to the consensus or composite result.

- **Individual Reviewer Comments.** Provides a means for reviewers to provide a brief comment back to the developers. This can be particularly useful if the reviewer has one or more solutions or recommendations that might be of value to the developers.

Access Permissions (Group of Fields). This group of fields consists of:

- Owner

- Group

- World

Each of these fields contains one of the following three values:

- Read and Write

- Read Only

- Access Denied

This information can be used to control who has access to viewing and/or altering the information contained on the template. If your database or environment already provides for security, you do not need these fields. Otherwise you can begin to impose at least a nominal level of security (particularly to prevent accidental change) through the use of this group of fields. Note that if the Assigned To group of fields is empty, then, in principle, no one can access this template until the process database administrator provides a name or group to the Assigned To fields. This can be avoided by assigning completed templates to (for instance) the SEPG leader's name. This allows others in the SEPG group to retain access and also permits the SEPG leader to reassign the template or adjust permissions as necessary.

Project Invocation ID. If you are building an environment that will automatically execute, manage, and control your processes and the flow of information and products through the processes, then an invocation identifier is important. To enact a process model typically involves "instantiating" a tailored subset of templates, which define the process to be followed by a specific project. To distinguish this unique instantiation, each template will need to have a Project Invocation ID that identifies the project using this instantiation of the process.

5.5.2 Activity Templates

So far, this book has discussed universal information inherited from the foundation template. This section turns to fields of information that specifically apply to only a single type of template: activity templates.

Only two types of information need to be captured on activity templates: model-specific information and end-product-related information. Since management-specific information is invariably applicable across all templates, it exists entirely on the foundation template and is a part of every template. For activity templates, all the fields in Section 5.5.2 are model specific with the exception of Elaboration Text fields in the Related Products and Related Supports groups of fields. Elaboration Text fields are end-product specific.

5.5.2.1 *Activity Criteria and Process (Group of Fields)*

The Activity Criteria and Process group of fields provides information about when the activity may start, the tasks or steps involved in the activity, when that activity may end, and conditions that must remain true for the activity to remain active. These fields are:

- **Objective.** An open text field used to augment the information in the Description or Purpose group of fields (inherited from the foundation template). Typically, this is a more concise representation of that information and specifically focuses on the objective of the activity.

- **Entry Criteria.** Explains the criteria that must be satisfied before an activity may begin. Typically, this information conveys that other activities must first be completed or certain products and resources must be available. However, this is a text field, so there are no restrictions on the type of information conveyed or on the manner in which it is conveyed. The goal is to explain as clearly and succinctly as possible, using natural language, the circumstances that allow the given activity to begin.

- **Internal Process.** Explains what the activity consists of and, at lower levels in the process model, how the activity is performed. This is not a formal description but a succinct natural language description of the activity. This field may become quite lengthy. If so, consider the advantages of establishing two or more child templates and moving some of the detail information to them.

- **Exit Criteria.** Explains the criteria that must be satisfied before the activity is considered complete. In the vast majority of cases, this will be in terms of finished products having been produced, inspected or reviewed, and, perhaps, baselined and placed under configuration management.

- **Invariants.** Used to capture information about things that must remain true for the activity to continue. Invariants differ from entry criteria, which are required to be true only at the time the activity starts; invariants must remain true throughout the activity. Examples of invariants: "Weekly status reports must be compiled and archived" or "Research continues only until the allocated funding is exhausted."

- **Abstraction Level.** To facilitate collecting sets of templates that contain, for instance, very detailed "how-to" steps or very high-level policy statements. These can then be referenced by other templates, at different levels of abstraction, with the confidence that the desired level of detail is available. You should distinguish the following five levels of activity abstractions:

  - **Process.** An activity that does not have discreet start and stop times but instead is ongoing. For example, "management" can be described as a process, whereas "review resumés" can be an activity.
  - **Activity.** Activities have start and stop times but typically lack "how-to" details.
  - **Methods.** Sequences of steps that describe, virtually in cookbook style, how to accomplish a particular task. Methods may involve one or more techniques.
  - **Techniques.** Practices that are generically useful but usually are combined with other techniques in order to build a "stand-alone" methodology.
  - **Examples.** Examples indicate templates that provide examples of how to do work.

5.5.2.2 Formal Activity Criteria and Process (Group of Fields)

This set of fields is similar to the Activity Criteria and Process group of fields except for one key difference: formality. Whereas the Activity Criteria and Process group of fields contains text-based information intended to be read and understood easily by humans, the Formal Activity Criteria and Process group of fields contains information that can be easily read and understood by computers. Whether you use a process programming language, state transition language, first-order predicate logic, or some other alternative or hybrid is a function of the capability of the enactment tool you are using. Use these fields to capture information that can be exported for use by an enactment tool:

- Entry Criteria

- Internal Process

- Exit Criteria

- Invariants

5.5.2.3 *Related Products (Group of Fields)*

For each activity there will typically be one or more products needed or produced by that activity. This group of fields captures product-related information:

- **Unique ID** (*multiple occurrence*). Contains the unique identifier of a product template.

- **Usage.** Provides information about when a particular product is needed by an activity. The three following options give a general indication of when a product must be made available to or exist within a given activity:
  - **Before Starting.** The product is an input, making that product part of the entry criteria for the activity.
  - **While Underway.** The activity can start without the product's being available and may end without the product, but sometime within the span of that activity, the product is necessary.
  - **Before Ending.** The product must exist before the activity can be considered done, thereby making that product part of the exit criteria for the activity.

- **Impact.** Conveys the primary impact this activity has on the product. This field contains one of the following four values:
  - **Left Unchanged.** Although the particular product is needed, it is not altered by this activity. As an example, an inspection process needs the artifact or product to be inspected and then releases it back to the author for any necessary updates (hence, changes occur outside the inspection process).
  - **Created.** This activity does not expect the product to be provided by prior work but instead creates that product, or at least the first parts of that product, itself. Although a product that has no subproducts, or children, will have only one activity that creates it, a complex product (with, possibly, several layers of subproducts) typically will be created in a variety of activities.
  - **Changed.** A version of the product was passed into this activity, and this activity updates, alters, extends, or otherwise changes the product before the end of the activity.
  - **Destroyed.** The product will be dismantled, consumed, disposed of, or otherwise made unavailable to all other activities within the process.
  - **Internal.** At higher levels of abstraction, a product that was created in one child might be changed in another child and destroyed in yet another child. In such cases, the value of Internal indicates that the entire existence of the product occurs inside this activity.

When the same product is used differently by the subactivities of an activity template, use the following conventions:
- If usages include both Left Unchanged and Changed, at the next higher level, indicate usage as Changed.
- If usages include both Created and Changed, use Created.
- If usages include both Changed and Destroyed, use Destroyed.
- If usages include both Created and Destroyed, use Internal.

Also note that there are logical relationships that exist between the values of the Usage and Impact fields. For instance, it is illogical if the Impact field indicates a product is created, but the Usage field indicates that product is needed before starting. Similarly, it is illogical for Usage to require a product to be in existence for the activity to end, with Impact indicating that the product is destroyed as part of the activity.

- **Tailoring Options.** Contains information about whether the product is, for instance, required or optional within this activity. These tailoring options allow for plans to be built from the process model that are tailored to the circumstances of particular projects. The values for this field are as follows. The meaning of these terms is consistent with their usage in Section 5.5.1.1. However, the relationship now specifically binds activities and products.
  - **Required.** The activity requires this particular product; there is not an option to tailor it out. Note that the usage field contains information about whether the product is required before the activity can begin, while the activity is underway, or before the activity can be considered done.
  - **Recommended.** The product is typically expected, used within, created, updated, or otherwise involved with the activity, but there is a waiver procedure available where a justification for excluding that product from the activity can be evaluated and possibly approved.
  - **Suggested.** It is within the authority of those planning or managing the project to use their own judgment about whether that particular product is important to their use of the activity within a particular project. Generally, Suggested products are included in project plans unless there is a compelling reason to exclude them. However, they may be excluded at discretion and without going through a waiver process.
  - **Optional.** The particular product is not typically included in project plans, but the person or persons planning or managing the project should be aware that these product options exist. Those persons may, at their own discretion, elect to include one of more of these optional products.

- **Restricted.** The opposite of Recommended. If you want to produce or use this particular product, you will have to go through a waiver process to be exempt from the policy that states not to use or make the product.
- **Prohibited.** The activity is not to use or produce this product. No waivers exist.

- **Source.** Used to distinguish where a product originates from. The suggested values for this field are:
  - **External.** Any product coming to an activity directly from outside the process.
  - **Internal.** A product that is generated as output from a prior activity in the process.

- **Destination.** Indicates where products go after this activity is done. The values for this field are:
  - **External**
  - **Internal**

  Use these terms as described under the Source field.

- **Purpose.** Gives some idea of why the activity needs that product. Example values for this field are:
  - **Development**. The activity participates in developing the product.
  - **Evaluation**. The activity is reviewing or auditing the product but otherwise leaving it alone.
  - **Reference.** The product is being used as a reference or example, and hence, the product in some way influences, but is not changed by, the activity.

- **Product Level of Quality Needed**. Used to indicate the degree of quality that must exist in a product before it is usable by this activity. For instance, early prototype activities can likely tolerate lower quality requirements. However, activities typically require higher-quality requirements as they become more development-oriented. This field can be especially useful when modeling "spiral" processes. Suggested field values are:
  - **Very Low**
  - **Low**
  - **Medium**
  - **High**
  - **Very High**

  Clearly, the assumption is that these levels are qualitative, as opposed to quantitative, values.

- **Product Criticality**. A field that ranges from Very Low to Very High (as described under Product Level of Quality Needed), indicating how critical this product is to the activity. During process simulation or enactment, this allows you to define, evaluate, and enforce complex heuristics for activity entry and exit criteria. These heuristics would, for example, evaluate the criticality of a product, in combination with its quality, to determine whether that product is ready to be used by the activity.

- **Elaboration Text.** Allows you to describe how the particular product relates specifically to this activity. Although the product template will contain general information about the product itself, the importance or application of that product within various activities will be different. Any important product-related information not already reflected in other fields is placed in the Elaboration Text field.

5.5.2.4 Related Support (Group of Fields)

In the basic templates, the Related Support group of fields is used to capture the roles involved in performing the activity:

- **Unique ID** (*multiple occurrence*). Contains the unique identifier of a role template.

- **Usage**. Indicates when a particular role is needed by an activity. The values of this field are exactly the same as explained in Section 5.5.2.3. However, the only time a role would be shown as not being needed until Before Ending is if that role is involved only in some type of quality assurance, sign-off, or other capacity that occurs only when, as far as the developers are concerned, the work is done and the activity is ready to end.

- **Tailoring Options**. Described in Section 5.5.2.3; contains the possible values of Required, Recommended, Optional, Suggested, Restricted, and Prohibited. The use of these terms is consistent in both groups of fields, except that here you are indicating whether the role is required, optional, and so forth, with respect to the activity.

- **Elaboration Text**. Similar to the Elaboration Text field for the Related Products group of fields. Allows you to state the particular responsibilities of the indicated role. General role information should be captured on the role template; this field is intended only to capture how the role specifically applies to or participates in this activity.

- **Minimum Required**. A cardinality field used to indicate the minimum number of resources or roles required to support the activity.

- **Preferred Allocation**. An ideal or preferred level of support, in terms of number of people, tools, or resources.

- **Maximum Allowed**. Any nonzero value in the Maximum Allowed field indicates the maximum number of resources or roles allowed.

- **Shared Access Needed**. A value that ranges from 0 to 100%; indicates an estimate of how much of the time the activity needs the support on a shared basis.

- **Exclusive Access Needed**. A value that ranges from 0 to 100%; indicates an estimate of how much of the time the activity needs the support on an exclusive basis.

- **Level of Support Efficiency Needed**. Used to indicate the degree of efficiency that is expected from the role or resources when it is applied to this activity. As before, with product quality, you should use a system with five efficiency levels: Very Low, Low, Medium, High, and Very High.

- **Support Criticality**. A field that ranges from Very Low to Very High, indicating how critical this support is to the activity. As with product criticality, this allows for complex heuristics about activity entry and exit criteria.

  The Duration Information fields assume that the Level of Support Efficiency Needed is provided. When efficiency levels are less than what is needed, your calculation (or simulation) of span or duration times should be proportionately increased. Similarly, higher levels of efficiency should result in shorter simulated durations. Use the Support Criticality field to adjust how much you allow the efficiency of a particular support to affect the duration time of the activity. The efficiency of a support with very high criticality should have considerably more influence on an activity's duration than the efficiency of a support with very low criticality.

- **Current Access Type**. Indicates the type of "lock" the activity currently has on the support. The two values are:
  - Shared
  - Exclusive. The role, tool, or resource is not currently available for use by any other.

5.5.2.5 Risks (Group of Fields)

It can be very useful to model the various risk factors that apply to activities. The fields that compose this group are:

- **Unique ID**. A unique identifier from a risk template.

- **Maximum Risk Tolerance**. A number, typically less than 1, that indicates how much risk you are willing to tolerate before corrective action is taken.

- **Applies To**. Indicates to which phase of the activity the risk applies:
  - Entry
  - Internal Process
  - Exit
  - All

- **Risk Likelihood**. A number from 0 to 1 indicating how likely you think this risk will manifest.

- **Risk Severity**. A number from 0 to 1 indicating the consequences of this risk's occurring. Generally values closer to 0 indicate low severity, and values approaching 1 indicate disaster.

- **Risk Frequency**. Reflects how often you expect this particular type of risk to recur. This value represents how often you think the risk is likely to occur on a per-cycle basis. Twice per cycle is frequency 2.0. A likelihood of once every couple of cycles indicates a frequency of 0.5. This refers to process risk, not product risk. Since processes have behavior in time, the risks associated with those processes also have time characteristics. When all else is equal, a risk that threatens weekly is distinctly different from one that threatens annually.

- **Elaboration Text**. A free text field that allows you to describe characteristics of the risk and how they specifically apply to this activity.

- **Current Risk Likelihood**. A fluctuating value that reflects your current best assessment of risk exposure as the project work occurs.

- **Current Risk Severity**. Reflects any changes to your impression of how severe a given risk is. Keep in mind that these represent actual evaluations as opposed to those used during process definition or project planning.

- **Current Risk Frequency**. Shows the current evaluation, as a project progresses, of how frequently you think a risk exposure will occur.

- **Delta Below Maximum Tolerance**. A calculated field. Its value is:

  Maximum risk tolerance – (risk likelihood • risk severity • frequency)

  If this calculation results in a negative number, you have exceeded your risk tolerance.

5.5.2.6 Constraints (Group of Fields)

Constraints are anything that influences your process but are not better represented using one of the other template classes. For instance, you might want to capture the fact that an activity must be compliant to a particular standard. You may find it clarifies your model to represent standards as constraints. This group of fields consists of:

- **Unique ID** (*multiple occurrence*). The unique identifier of a constraint template.

- **Applies To.** Indicates which part of an activity is subject to the constraint. Options for this field are:
  - Entry
  - Internal Process
  - Exit
  - All

- **Elaboration Text**. Allows you to describe specifically, in free text, how the constraint applies to this activity.

- **Currently In Effect**. Indicates whether the constraint is currently active. Keep in mind that internal constraints are those for which you can receive a waiver. If the constraint has been waived, it is no longer in effect. Values for this field are:
  - Yes
  - No
  - Partially

5.5.2.7 Activity State Information (Group of Fields)

If you intend to use your process information to drive a process simulation or as a foundation for an automated enactment environment, state information (especially for activities) can allow for more subtle or granular heuristics. This group of fields consists of:

- **State System Identifier** (*multiple occurrence*). A unique identifier for a set of states. For any given activity, it may be subject to two or more systems of state transitions. For example, there may be one system of states that represents activity transitions from an engineering perspective, another that represents activity transitions from a management perspective, and still another used to define activity transitions from an auditor's perspective. Keep in mind that complexity in a process model invariably introduces risk of misunderstanding, mismodeling, and miscommunication. Therefore, you should create multiple state systems only when doing so simplifies, as opposed to complicates, your model.

- **Label** (*multiple occurrence*). The unique identifier for a particular activity within a cohesive set of states within one state system. You will need a unique label for each distinct state within that state system.

- **Description.** Describes the state.

- **Application.** Indicates whether this set of states should be used only at the current level of abstraction, or whether it is passed through inheritance to all the children (at all sublevels) under this template. The values for this field are:
  - Node Only
  - All Children

- **Augments.** A yes-no field that is relevant only when a set of states has been inherited and when different state information is available at this level. A value of No indicates the local state information completely replaces any inherited information. A value of Yes indicates that the local set of states extends or augments the inherited set.

- **Current Activity State(s).** Indicates in an ongoing enactment of the process what the current state is of this particular activity. If you have defined multiple state systems, then this is a set of fields—one field for each state system.

5.5.2.8 Process Quality Attributes (Group of Fields)

Depending on your needs, values for the following fields can be qualitative or quantitative. Keep in mind that these are process quality fields:

- Reliability

- Efficiency

- Effectiveness

- Predictability

- Safety

- Error Density

- Fault Tolerance

- Probable Correctness

- Availability

- Maintainability

- Evolvability

- Security

- Survivability

- Utility

As with other qualitative judgments, we recommend that, at most, you use a five-level scale: Very Low, Low, Medium, High, and Very High. By rating activities using some or all of these attributes, you allow for choosing between process options as a function of these attributes and their relative importance to a particular project.

For consistency, you set these fields only at final templates and heuristically derive appropriate values for any contributing templates. Generally, span or duration times of child activities can be used to weight the emphasis given to a child's attributes.

5.5.2.9 Duration Information (Group of Fields)

This group of fields is used to capture the duration of an activity. This information is essential if you want to investigate simulated execution of your process. You will want to adapt this set of fields to match the conventions used by your simulation environment. However, example information needed by many tools includes average duration and how much this activity varies from the average. Certainly, standard deviations can be used. However, you can allow for more unbalanced variation by using lower and upper "high confidence" thresholds, as shown in the following list:

- Average Duration

- Typically More Than

- Typically Less Than

5.5.2.10 Planned and Actuals (Group of Fields)

This group of fields provides a means to capture both what you plan for an activity and what actually occurs:

- Planned Earliest Start

- Planned Latest Start

- Planned Earliest Finish

- Planned Latest Finish

- Actual Start

- Percent Complete

- Actual Finish

- Critical Path

The earliest and latest start and finish fields support project planning and enactment. Of course, actuals can vary from planned, so there are fields to capture actual start and stop dates. Percent Complete is a value that ranges from 0 to 100 and can be used to facilitate analysis of project progress. Note that at the final templates, this information needs to be provided by someone. On any contributing template, it can be calculated as a function of weighted percent completion of the children. Critical Path can be derived algorithmically and contains either a Yes or No value.

5.5.3 Activity/Decision Templates

This class of templates is used to represent the key decision points of your process. At a minimum, we recommend you collect additional information that characterizes the source(s) of information used to support the decision process. Note that the decision template is actually a special form of the activity template. Therefore, this template inherits (or includes) all the field values from the activity, and adds the possibility of more activity details, or fields, that specifically characterize or are important to decision-making activities.

5.5.3.1 *Source of Information, Planned (Group of Fields)*

The following fields contribute to evaluating the source of information on which the decision is based:

- Source Unique ID (*multiple occurrence*)

- Expected Declared Accuracy of Information

- Expected Reliability of Source

- Expected Timeliness of Information

- Elaboration Text

Expected Declared Accuracy of Information represents what you expect to be the source's evaluation of the accuracy of the information. For example, you might typically expect a source of information to consider its information to be 95% accurate.

Expected Reliability of Source represents the confidence level you typically associate with that source of information.

Expected Timeliness of Information is a five-tier scale:

Very Untimely

Somewhat Untimely

Questionable Timeliness

Somewhat Timely

Very Timely

As a rule, the more untimely information is, the less useful it is.

5.5.3.2 Source of Information, Actual (Group of Fields)

- Source Unique ID (*multiple occurrence*)

- Declared Accuracy of Information

- Reliability of Source

- Timeliness of Information

These fields are direct counterparts to those described in Section 5.5.3.1. The only difference is that, in advanced applications, you want to compare real-world values with those you had planned.

5.5.3.3 Minimum Threshold for Decision (Group of Fields)

There are two fields in this group:

- Text Description

- Numeric Minimum

Generally you at least want to be able to describe, using the Text Description field, the minimum standards on accuracy, reliability, and timeliness of information for the decision process to occur. For either simulation or enactment, you will also need to use the Numeric Minimum field.

5.5.4 Activity/Production Templates

This class of templates is used to represent directly billable activities. Consequently, this template adds a field to capture charge code information.

5.5.4.1 Project Charge Code

Although you might find this field valuable at lower tiers of usage, for project enactment, you will want to capture the charge codes to which activities are billed.

5.5.5 Activity/Milestone Templates

Milestone templates are used to highlight key events within the process model. It is recommended that you use the convention that milestones are events, and, hence, they do not take any time to occur. This can be easily represented using only the exit criteria fields on this template.

5.5.6 Activity/Overhead Templates

Overhead templates are the counterpart of production templates. There are no project-direct charge codes for these activities.

5.5.7 Activity/Corrective Action Templates

The corrective action class of templates is used to highlight how you recover from problems. The use of these templates is exactly like the use of Exception Handlers in Ada. For simulation purposes, if a problem (such as noncompliant product) manifests within an activity, that activity should have a mechanism for addressing the problem. If not, the problem "propagates" to the next higher level. Ideally, at some point your process has a "corrective action" mechanism for handling the problem in a planned and predictable manner.

5.5.8 Activity/Quality Assurance Templates

Quality assurance has different meanings for different people. However you use this template, be sure to define, on the foundation quality assurance template, exactly what your organization considers the scope of quality assurance to be. If you have different types of quality assurance activities, use the Type field described in Section 5.5.8.1.

5.5.8.1 *Type*

As a simple example, different types of quality assurance activities may be:

- Desk Check

- Sample

- Review

- Inspection

In general, this list moves from activities that typically are more subjective to those that are more objective. If you do not elect to use the Audit templates (discussed in Section 5.5.10), you can capture audit activities as a fifth type of quality assurance activity.

5.5.9 Activity/Configuration Management Templates

Use this template to highlight and define activities related to the configuration management process. As with other class-level templates, you may find it useful to distinguish different types of configuration management (as a function of "what" is going through the configuration management process).

5.5.9.1 *Type*

Some organizations have different types of configuration management. Often this is a function of the product. For instance, the configuration management process for plans may be fundamentally different from that for noncompliant products. Unless you essentially do only one type of configuration management, you should distinguish these activities by type—for example:

- Plan Control

- Design Control

- Product Control

- Noncompliant Product Control

5.5.10 Activity/Audit Templates

Use this template to highlight audit activities. Clearly distinguish why some activities are quality assurance, and other activities are audits. Typically the term audit indicates an investigation by an outside or totally independent entity.

5.5.11 Activity/Process Improvement Templates

These templates can be used to emphasize activities specifically related to process improvement. Although not shown here, you may also want to include a "motivation" field for indicating, for example, whether this activity is CMM motivated, Malcolm Baldrige motivated, ISO 9000 motivated, or internally motivated. Allow for the fact that a single activity may be motivated by two or more quality initiatives.

5.5.11.1 Type

Process improvement is often conducted according to a relatively standard sequence of life-cycle phases. You may find it useful to distinguish process improvement activities as a function of which phase that activity supports—for example:

- Process Improvement Process Research
- Assessment for Process Improvement
- Planning Process Improvement
- Implementing Process Improvement Support Products
- Piloting Process Improvement
- Technology Transfer
- Monitoring Process Improvement

5.5.12 Activity/Training Templates

Use this class of templates to define activities related to training. Note that the results of these activities are often intangible. You can model the output of training by using the Product/Intangible/Skill template.

5.5.13 Activity/Purchasing Templates

Use this template whenever purchased products or services are an important part of the process.

5.5.14 Activity/Service Templates

This template is for service that you provide to others, not service they provide to you. Most commonly, use this template to capture how you service one or more products produced by the process.

5.5.15 Activity/Documentation Templates

Often the development of a product entails the creation and delivery of a considerable amount of documentation. Use this template to highlight activities dedicated to documentation development.

5.5.16 Activity/Measurement Templates

Measurement templates are used to show where, when, and how metrics are collected within your process.

5.5.16.1 Type

- Product
- Process
- General

Typically, you can divide metrics into those that measure product characteristics and those that measure process characteristics. If you find if difficult to classify a metric into these two distinctions, then indicate it as a general metric. For the purposes of this template, there is no distinction between "measures" and "metrics." Either or both can be documented using this template.

5.5.16.2 Collection

You will likely want to show measurement activities as collecting more than one measure or metric. This collection of fields repeats for each different measure or metric you collect—for example:

- Metric ID (*multiple occurrence*)
- Unit of Measure
- Method of Collection
- Frequency of Collection
- Collected By

The primary purpose of this group of fields is to ensure consistency in how and how often metrics are collected.

5.5.16.3 Recorded In

Use this field to show where the metric information is stored—for example, a report or database. Your process should also show where, when, and how the metric information is used.

5.5.17 Product Templates

Product templates contain information about the characteristics, purpose, and use of products within the overall process model. In addition to the fields inherited from the foundation template, the product templates add a few fields that capture details about products in particular and the activities to which these products are related.

5.5.17.1 Quality Rating Levels (Group of Fields)

- Quality Level/Unique ID (*multiple occurrence*)
- Quality Level Description
- Current Product Level of Quality

The Current Product Level of Quality field uses the same levels as described in Product Level of Quality Needed. This field permits distinguishing between what is needed and what exists.

5.5.17.2 *State Information (Group of Fields)*

These fields are of interest primarily if you plan to use a relatively formal graphical nota
tion, such as IDEF, to portray process information. Until you have a particular need to
reference state information, there is little reason to attempt to define it. Conversely, it is
often convenient, particularly in entry and exit criteria fields, to be able to refer to a product as being in a particular state. When you establish and define a set of states for a product,
it becomes far easier for everyone to use a common vocabulary when referring to the various transitions that a product typically goes through. This group of fields is composed of:

- **State System Identifier** (*multiple occurrence*). As with activity states, the
  unique identifier for a set of states. Any product may be subject to two or
  more systems of state transitions. Complexity in a process model invariably
  introduces risk; you should create multiple state systems only when doing so
  simplifies your model.

- **Label** (*multiple occurrence*). The unique identifier which is the name of the
  state.

- **Description**. A brief explanation of the characteristics or boundaries of the state.

- **Application**. When you define one or more systems of states for a product,
  any one set, or state system, may apply only to that template or may also
  apply to all the children of that template. The Application field reflects this
  scope through the following two values:
  – Node Only
  – All Children

- **Augments**. A yes-no field that is relevant only when a set of states has been
  inherited and when different state information is available at this level. A
  value of No indicates the local state information completely replaces any
  inherited information. A value of Yes indicates that the local set of states
  extends or augments the inherited set.

- **Current Product State(s)**. Indicates, in an ongoing enactment of the process,
  the current state of this particular product. If you have defined multiple state
  systems, this would be a set of fields—one field for each state system.

The following list is an example of types of states you might want to define for a particular
product:

1. Planned

2. Scheduled

3. Authorized

4. Enabled

5. Under Development

    a. Phase 1 Completed

    b. Phase 2 Completed

    c. Phase N Completed

6. Ready for Review

7. Reserved for Review

8. Under Review

9. Review Completed

10. In Rework

11. Completed

12. In Suspension

13. Cancelled

14. Approved

15. Released

Other possiblities are:

16. Fielded

17. Planned for Retirement

18. Scheduled for Retirement

19. Being Retired

20. Retired

The purpose, use, and development of products vary widely as a function of the product itself, so it is highly unlikely that a single set of states works equally well for all the various types of products you represent in your model. Consequently, it is useful to allow for different sets of state information, where each set is applicable to one or more different classes of products.

It is worth repeating that the effort to identify and define state information should be made only when you are confident that this information has sufficient value and will actually be used.

5.5.17.3 Related Activities (Multiple Occurrence)

This field contains the unique identifiers of all activities to which the product is related. A product is related to an activity if the activity needs, uses, references, alters, or otherwise expects the availability of that product in any way.

5.5.17.4 Risks (Group of Fields)

This set of fields is exactly like activity risks, except that the risks are product specific. Consequently, the values appropriate for the Applies To field are different. The fields that constitute this group are:

- Unique ID (*multiple occurrence*)
- Maximum Risk Tolerance
- Applies To
- Elaboration Text
- Risk Likelihood
- Risk Severity
- Risk Frequency
- Current Risk Likelihood
- Current Risk Severity
- Current Risk Frequency
- Delta Below Maximum Tolerance

Applies To, for product risks, takes one of the following values:

- Creation
- Development
- Maintenance
- Usage
- Retirement
- Destruction
- All

Use the Applies To field to associate the risk you are describing with one of the principal life-cycle phases of the product.

5.5.17.5 Constraints (Group of Fields)

Use this field to show how constraints relate to this product. This group consists of the following fields:

- Unique ID (*multiple occurrence*)
- Applies To
- Elaboration Text
- Currently In Effect

Use this field to describe constraints as they might affect various life-cycle phases of the product.

5.5.17.6 Source and Destination (Group of Fields)

Sometimes you can trace the origination of a product to a single activity. Also, its destination may be a single activity. If so, you can use these fields to capture that information:

- Origination
- Destination

These fields contain either a unique activity identifier or the word External. Typically, all delivered products show External as their destination. However, some products you use may also have an external origination.

5.5.18 Product/Tangible Product Template

Product templates have two major classes: tangible and intangible. Tangible products are of various types, and the fields in Section 5.5.18.1 and 5.5.18.2 can be used to indicate the primary type of product this is. Keep in mind that this information is used to augment the information collected for all products in general. These particular augmentations apply specifically to tangible products (and all subclasses of tangible products).

5.5.18.1 Type

- Developed Product
- Value-added Product

- Purchaser Supplied Product

- Measurement Product

- Plans

- Policies and Procedures

- Standards

Product types are highly dependent on business domain, customers, market, and so forth. Tailor the list of types to suit your specific circumstances.

5.5.18.2 Security Classification

Products from your process may need to be characterized by a security designation—for example, public, company proprietary, secret, top secret, or classified. In an elaborate enactment or simulation model, ensure that the roles or people assigned to an activity have the appropriate clearance levels to access the products provided to or generated by that activity.

5.5.19 Product/Tangible Product/Contract Deliverable Template

One of the most important product distinctions is whether a product will be delivered to a customer. If it will be, use this template for detailed product information.

5.5.20 Product/Tangible Product/Contract Nondeliverable Template

If a product is not intended for delivery to a customer or client but is required by the contract, use this template. If you do not need to highlight the distinction between delivered and nondelivered products, use the Destination field at the meta-class level to capture this distinction. Otherwise, your selection of this subclass template must be consistent with the value of the Destination field.

5.5.21 Product/Tangible Product/Noncontract Nondeliverable Template

Use this template to represent any products generated or used during the process that are not required by the contract and not delivered to the customer. For example, your process might require that you design and develop custom software to test and evaluate the performance of products required by the contract. If the contract does not require you to build that custom software and you do not intend to release it to the customer, represent it with this template.

5.5.22 Product/Tangible Product/Status Reports

If status reports do not require high visibility within your process, you do not need this template. Instead, you can simply add "status reports" as one of the tangible product types listed in Section 5.5.18.1. However, there are a variety of reasons that you might want to highlight explicitly the generation and use of status reports within your process. For example, you can use status reports as the critical mechanism that controls your process. In such a model, status reports are used to convey the states of products and activities, product quality, and so forth. An activity would then look to various status reports to determine whether it can execute or continue executing, and may itself generate one or more status reports during execution or at completion.

If you use this template, and if some status reports are required as contract deliverable, and others are noncontract, nondeliverable, you will need a Type field on this template to capture those distinctions.

5.5.23 Product/Intangible Product Template

Aside from tangible products, there are also intangible products. Intangible products result from activities occurring that yield value to you or your customer but do not necessarily produce something tangible. The two primary examples of intangible products are knowledge and skills.

5.5.24 Product/Intangible Product/Knowledge Templates

When an activity involves the accumulation of important information but does not result in any documentation of that information, use the knowledge template to show how this "product" (knowledge) is both generated and used.

5.5.25 Product/Intangible Product/Skill Templates

Skill templates are one of the most common "output products" of training activities.

5.5.25.1 *Proficiency Rating Levels (Group of Fields)*

In addition to the efficiency fields inherited from the support template, role templates can also show roles at different levels of proficiency. Proficiency ratings on this skill template indicate the different levels of ability you may need for a role to have at various times or places within your process. This group of fields consists of:

- **Proficiency Level/Unique ID** (*multiple occurrence*). Each Proficiency Level needs a unique identifier. Use the following scale:
  - Academic
  - Trained
  - Novice
  - Experienced
  - Highly Experienced
  - Expert

  Role templates will use these values to indicate how proficient a role needs to be at this and other skills.

- **Proficiency Level Description**. To explain the distinguishing characteristics of each level of proficiency.

5.5.26 Support Templates

Support templates include both roles and resources. As a very general guideline, roles apply only to people; all else that supports the process is considered a resource. Type of access, sharing, locks, and so forth become important at higher or more formal levels of usage.

5.5.26.1 *Type of Access Available*

For both roles and resources, it is necessary to know whether the support is available only in a shared capacity, only in an exclusive capacity, or both. Use the following field values to capture this information:

- Shared Only

- Exclusive Only

- Shared and Exclusive

5.5.26.2 Share (Group of Fields)

If a support is available in any type of a shared capacity, you need additional information. Use this group of fields to capture information on how sharing occurs:

- **Share Limit**. If a role, resource, or tool can be shared, it is sometimes the case it cannot be infinitely shared. Use the Share Limit field to put a limit on how many activities the support can be shared between.

- **Current Share Count**. Used to hold an actual count of the current number of "shared locks" on this role or resource. When Current Share Count equals Share Limit, the support cannot participate in any other shared support activities (until one or more activities that currently hold locks release them).

5.5.26.3 Security Clearance

If your process involves products that carry a security classification, then the Supports for your process may need to be characterized by a security clearance (none, company proprietary, secret, top secret, classified, etc.). The set of security levels used to characterize your products and supports needs to be consistent.

In addition to people having sufficient clearance to access a sensitive product, you might also need to apply this concept to other supports. That is, it may be that only certain copy machines may be used to duplicate classified material, that only particular rooms can be used when reviewing or discussing top-secret information, or that disposal of secret material must occur only in certain rooms or containers.

5.5.26.4 Supported Activities (Multiple Occurrence)

For every activity needing this support, it might be necessary if you are building an automated enactment environment to know what type of "lock" is held on the support. Generally, at any given moment, a support will have no locks on it, one exclusive lock and no other locks, or up to "share limit" shared locks. Additionally, at any moment there may be an arbitrary number of requests for locks pending from the various activities. The values for the Current Lock Status field are:

- Shared Lock Held
- Exclusive Lock Held
- Requesting Shared
- Requesting Exclusive

5.5.26.5 *Efficiency Rating (Group of Fields)*

Efficiency Rating for supports allows you to explore the implications of using more or less efficient roles or resources in supporting the various activities. This group of fields consists of:

- **Efficiency Level/Unique ID** (*multiple occurrence*). For each level of efficiency. Use a three- or five-step scale that ranges from (well-) below average to (well-) above average.

- **Efficiency Level Description**. Explains the distinguishing characteristics of this level of efficiency.

- **Efficiency Impact Multiplier**. Each activity has an average duration. However, you will want to make the estimated duration of an activity a function of the efficiency of the roles, tools, and resources assigned to that activity. An Efficiency Impact Multiplier of 1.0 has no impact on durations. Multipliers greater than 1 will result in longer durations and multipliers less than 1, shorter durations.

5.5.26.6 *Current Level of Support Efficiency*

During dynamic simulation or enactment, you may want to vary the efficiency of a support or otherwise tie the efficiency to a variety of other factors (e.g., reduce level of efficiency with each new "shared lock" on the support). Use this field to show the actual (as opposed to default) efficiency level. Although you can establish this field as a direct multiplier, it is recommended that you use an identifier from one of the efficiency levels in the Efficiency Rating group of fields instead (Section 5.5.26.5).

5.5.26.7 *Risks (Group of Fields)*

Risks associated to supports are similar, in how you define them, to risks associated with products or risks associated with activities. The following fields are identical to those named in activity risks and product risks. The only exception is that this group of fields does not contain the field Applies To. When you associate a risk with a support, it applies to that support in general.

- Unique ID (*multiple occurrence*)
- Maximum Risk Tolerance
- Elaboration Text

- Risk Likelihood
- Risk Severity
- Risk Frequency
- Current Risk Likelihood
- Current Risk Severity
- Current Risk Frequency
- Delta Below Maximum Tolerance

An example of support risk is Unavailability. For instance, if you expect normally not to have a role on staff but plan a process that presumes you can acquire the needed skills through hiring, then you may want to highlight that risk:assumption.

5.5.26.8 Support State Information (Group of Fields)

For advanced applications, you will find it useful to expand on the state information for supports and how to interpret that information by adding the following fields:

- State System Identifier (*multiple occurrence*)
- Label (*multiple occurrence*)
- Description
- Application
- Augments
- Current State(s)

The use of these fields is similar to the descriptions provided in activity states and product states.

5.5.27 Support/Role Templates

Role templates are used to show how humans are involved in the process. With roles, it is important to capture information about reporting structures; skill proficiencies; authority; and, in highly advanced applications, who within the organization is qualified to hold which roles.

5.5.27.1 Reports To

This group of fields reflects those roles to which this particular role reports. This information is composed of:

- **Unique ID** (*multiple occurrence*). Contains the unique identifier of another role template.

- **Elaboration Text**. Contains clarifying information about this particular reporting relationship, such as what is reported and how often.

In virtually all role structures, there is an implicit reporting path from child templates to parent templates. However, it is highly recommended that you explicitly capture that reporting structure using the Reports To fields (even though it is implied by the Parent field). The Reports To fields are also used to define any reporting paths not implied by parent-child relationships.

At higher levels of abstraction, this field is not always applicable. For instance, if you model an inspection team as a role, then typically the entire team does not report to someone. Instead, the team reports to the moderator, and the moderator has reporting responsibilities outside the team.

5.5.27.2 Reported To By

This field shows the other half of the reporting relationships. Specifically, it contains the unique identifiers of any other role templates that report to this role.

At higher levels of abstraction, the role may not represent a person, and the concept of being reported to is not applicable. There are also exceptions. For example, "Board of Directors" can be modeled as a "complex" role, with the "CEO" role reporting to it.

5.5.27.3 Unique Individual

This is a yes-no field that indicates whether the template is being used to represent a specific and real individual within the organization. If this is truly a role, and not a real person, the field value is No; otherwise, use Yes.

5.5.27.4 Proficiency (Group of Fields)

Skill templates (a subclass of intangible products) are used to show skill as an output product of training. Roles need certain skills. Use this group of fields to show the skill levels necessary for this role. The fields in this group are:

- **Required Skill Area Unique ID** (*multiple occurrence*). The unique identifier of a skill template.

- **Minimum Level of Proficiency**. The skill template defines a group of fields that define the different levels of proficiency, or expertise, that apply to the skill. Select one of those levels of proficiency to represent the Minimum Level of Proficiency that must be achieved to have adequate skill in this area. If this role template is being used to the level of detail where it represents an actual person (that is, Unique Individual field has a value of Yes), then the semantics of this field is not "minimum" level of proficiency but "actual" level of proficiency.

- **Required Skill Area Elaboration Text**. Provides a text explanation about the use or importance of the skill to the role.

5.5.27.5 Internal Constraint Waiver Authority (Group of Fields)

If you use internal constraint templates, the implication is that some role exists that has the authority to waive the constraint:

- **Template Unique ID** (*multiple occurrence*). Use to list the identifier(s) of internal constraint templates for which this role has waiver authority.

- **Waiver Elaboration Text**. Use to provide any details or additional information about the nature of or conditions surrounding when, why, or how a waiver occurs.

5.5.27.6 Approved Staff Unique ID (Multiple Occurrence)

If this template represents a role, as opposed to an actual person, then list all the identifiers of actual persons approved to hold this role. When the role template represents a real person, this field is meaningless and left blank.

5.5.28 Support/Tool Templates

Use the tool template to highlight the primary tools that participate in the process. Note that if a tool involves a network site license that limits simultaneous use to, for instance, eight people, then you will want to set the field Share Limit to 8.

5.5.29 Support/Resource Templates

Use this template to represent any resource needed to perform the process (training rooms, meeting rooms, various office supplies, etc.). Represent only those resources considered important in understanding, analyzing, or performing the process. This template adds only one field to those inherited.

5.5.29.1 Owned By

This field indicates ownership of resources. Whether you own a particular resource can have a significant impact on the types of risk you have with respect to that resource.

5.5.30 Constraint Templates

Constraint templates have two important uses: (1) to indicate any constraining influence that is not better represented as an activity, product, or support and (2) to simplify models. For instance, if you have 30 different entry criteria for a particular activity, you can clean your model by showing, for instance, a constraint that indicates "Task Manager decides activity may start."

These trade-offs always have a price. On one side you have detailed accuracy, but may lack clarity. On the other side, clarity is improved, but details are lost. At lower tiers, opt for improved clarity; at higher tiers, you will need the details.

If you find yourself using a high number of constraint templates (maybe, higher than 10% of your total templates) then examine the constraints and see if you can extract another meta-class. If so, your model will be more informative when you establish that meta-class and elaborate it with appropriate details.

You may have constraints on activities, products, and supports. Generally, however, if a constraint is applicable to products (for instance), it is applicable only to products. This is not a rule; it is just in the nature of constraints. If you have a constraint that applies to more than one meta-class, reexamine that constraint to be sure that you are not inadvertently using it to represent two different things. Additionally, the nature of the constraint may introduce risk.

5.5.30.1 *Constrained Activities (Multiple Occurrence)*

When the constraint applies to one or more activities, put the activity template unique identifiers in this field.

5.5.30.2 *Constrained Products (Multiple Occurrence)*

Use this field for unique identifiers of products subject to this constraint.

5.5.30.3 *Constrained Supports (Multiple Occurrence)*

If the constraint applies to roles, tools, resources, or other supports, put the support template identifiers in this field.

5.5.30.4 *Constraint Induced Risks (Group of Fields)*

The fields in this group are identical to those discussed in support risks. Because anything that influences your process can be modeled as a constraint, you may also find it useful to include the Applies To field in this group. Examples of its use can be found in activity risks and product risks.

5.5.31 Constraint/Internal Constraint Template

Internal constraint templates are used to represent any constraint where those who participate in the process have the option to receive a waiver to that constraint.

5.5.31.1 *Waiver Criteria*

Use this field to describe in detail the criteria that justify a waiver to this constraint.

5.5.31.2 *Roles Authorized to Exercise Waiver (Multiple Occurrence)*

The role templates show which internal constraints a role has waiver authority over. This field represents the opposite side of that view. That is, use this field to show which roles have waiver authority over this constraint. Your environment may automatically maintain this type of "reverse relation"; if so, you do not need this field.

5.5.32 Constraint/External Constraint Template

External constraints are constraints for which there are no waivers—for example, your organization's safety policies or standards.

5.5.33 Risk Template Meta-Class

The last meta-class of templates is used to represent risk. Each of the other meta-classes (activities, products, supports, and constraints) has fields to reflect the types of risk that may be associated with them. Use risk templates to capture details about these risks and their degrees of impact.

5.5.33.1 Severity Levels (Group of Fields)

Each risk should be divided into several levels, with each level indicating severity of impact. At a minimum, show two levels of risk (Moderate and Severe). At the other end of the spectrum, avoid using more than a seven-level table (ranging from Extremely Low to Extremely Severe). This group of fields consists of:

- Level/ID Number (*multiple occurrence*)
- Level Description. To explain how the severity of the consequences can be distinguished at each level.

5.5.33.2 Activity Risks Unique IDs (Multiple Occurrence)

This is a "reverse-relation" field that you may not need, depending on the automated environment you are using. For any activity template that indicates the activity is subject to this risk, show the activity's unique identifiers in this field.

5.5.33.3 Product Risks Unique IDs (Multiple Occurrence)

This too is a "reverse-relation" field. For any product template that indicates the product is subject to this risk, show the product's unique identifiers in this field.

5.5.33.4 *Support Risks Unique IDs (Multiple Occurrence)*

Use this field to establish the reverse relation from risks to support templates.

5.5.33.5 *Constraint Risks Unique IDs (Multiple Occurrence)*

This field contains identifiers for constraint templates that reference this risk template.

5.5.34 Risk/Cost Risk Template

Use this template whenever the primary impact of a risk is cost.

5.5.35 Risk/Quality Risk Template

Use this template to capture information about quality risk. If you use the performance and construction risk templates, exclude those characteristics from consideration as quality attributes. If you elect not to use performance and construction risk templates, consider those factors as relating to product quality and use this template.

5.5.35.1 *Type of Quality Risk*

At a minimum, quality risk can be divided into that which applies to products and that which applies to the process producing the products. In the event that a risk does not seem to apply clearly to products or activities, show it as a General risk:

- Product

- Process

- General

Typically, product risk will be mapped only to product templates, process risks will be mapped only to activities, and so forth, although there may be exceptions. When you encounter an exception, verify that you are accurately relating risks to the appropriate process objects.

5.5.36 Risk/Schedule Risk Template

Sometimes the primary consequence of a risk is its impact on schedule. Use this template to define these risks.

5.5.37 Risk/Performance Risk Template

The performance risk template is used to define product performance risk and process performance risk.

5.5.37.1 Performance Risk Applies To

As with the quality risk templates, this field can have one of three values:

- Product
- Process
- General

When the speed, throughput, or other performance characteristics of a product represent an important risk consideration, it is product risk; when the risk relates to how fast or efficiently activities are performed, show it as a process type of risk.

5.5.38 Risk/Construction Risk Template

This risk applies entirely to products. When you think that the quality of construction (as opposed to how a product performs) is at risk, use this template.

5.5.39 Risk/Predictability Risk Template

You will note, as you analyze and perform risk management, that there are certain common relationships that affect the risk trade-offs you make and their impact on your overall risk exposure. For example, by increasing the number of quality reviews within a process, you usually reduce quality risk but increase cost risk and schedule risk. Conversely, by eliminating some of the intermediate product inspections and tests, you might reduce schedule risk and cost risk but significantly increase quality risk.

Occasionally, you may elect to eliminate activities from a process in a way that at first seems to reduce cost risk, schedule risk, and quality risk and have no impact on performance risk or construction risk. Such "no-cost" improvements are exceedingly rare and should be viewed suspiciously. Often what you have lost is predictability in the outcome of your process. Uncertainty in a process is undesirable. When actions (or the lack of actions) adversely affect your confidence in meeting project plans, you can represent this using predictability risk templates.

5.6 SUMMARY

The more advanced your usage of process information is, the greater is the likelihood that information, and its relationship to other information, will be unique to your circumstances and needs. A few fields are generally applicable to all circumstances, environments, and business domains (activity entry criteria, for example, is almost universally useful). However, by the time you are implementing highly advanced applications and usage, the data you collect, their relative importance, and how you use that information will all depend extensively on your budget, the experience of your people, your organization's tactical and strategic goals, the relative dependence of those goals on process definitions and models, your organizational circumstances, and various other process drivers.

For successful process improvement, it is crucial for you to remember that process representation, like essentially all else in business, needs to be a profitable endeavor. The benefit derived from doing the work must exceed the cost of performing it, or it does not make business sense. Of course, cost and benefit should be considered in the largest sense of these words. Process improvement has easily measurable benefits, such as reduced activity cost and improved product quality, but it also has numerous other benefits, such as increased customer loyalty, enhanced organizational prestige, improved employee morale, and countless other advantages. Though the dollar impact of these benefits is hard to calculate, it's nonetheless quite real.

In closing, here is a final guideline you can use to gauge the likelihood of success for the process improvement program. As you help your organization with process improvement, if you're not enjoying your work, you're probably not doing it right.

ABBREVIATIONS AND ACRONYMS

CASE	computer-aided software engineering
CM	configuration management
CMM	capability maturity model
DOD	Department of Defense
ESP	evolutionary spiral process
ETVX	entry-task-validation-exit
FAA	Federal Aviation Administration
IDEF	integrated definition
IE	improvement efforts
ISO	International Organization of Standardization
MPDM	managed process definition methodology
NASA	National Aeronautics and Space Administration
NSA	National Security Agency
OPD	organizational process development
PAD	project application development
PASTA	process and artifact state transition abstraction
PAT	process action team
PERT	program evaluation and review technique
PLD	product-line-based product and process development
PPA	program process architecture
QA	quality assurance
R&D	research and development
RFP	request for proposal
RIN	role interaction nets
SADT	structured analysis and design technique
SDT	state transition diagram
SEI	Software Engineering Institute
SEPG	Software Engineering Process Group
SPICE	Software Process Improvement Capability Determination
TQM	total quality management
V&V	verification and validation
VCOE	Virginia Center of Excellence for Software Reuse and Technology Transfer

GLOSSARY

Class template	Derived from meta-class templates, with information unique to that template.
Constraint	Those things required to disable or prevent the wrong things from happening. Process constraints describe the limiting conditions associated with the activation, performance, or cessation of an event. In this guidebook, constraints have been divided into two general types: internal and external.
Contributing template	Any non-leaf-node templates.
Cycle	A traversal of all five sectors of the spiral model, which denotes that some aspect of the product has matured by a specific amount.
End product	The product that results from a process definition and modeling effort—for example: guidebooks, training material, subsections of proposals, operations manuals, project plans.
Estimate of the situation (EOS)	A document that identifies the project's goals, strategies, product and process assumptions, and assets available for performing a project.
External constraints	All factors that may limit or constrain how an activity proceeds, that are not directly attributable to local authority (which are modeled as internal constraints) —for example: quality requirements, corporate standards, division policies, engineering procedures, process guidelines, and management directives. External constraints differ from internal constraints in that they are typically not subject to discretionary use; they are intended to be, and expected to be, explicitly followed, regardless of project-specific issues.
Final template	The leaf-node templates.
Foundation template	All templates are derived from a common foundation template.

Guidance	The use of a process definition (constraint) by an observer or process agent to provide the enacting process agent with the legal set of process step options at any point of the enactment of the observed process. This may involve process cues, process interaction, or process management.
Internal constraints	Those constraints that you have authority to change, countermand, enforce, and so forth, typically managerial in nature and usually in the form of authority and permission—for example, management authority or permission required before an event can commence. Internal constraints also convey authority to roles to suspend events, cancel activities, recommence activities, cease activity, etc. Internal constraints are always coupled with a role (typically a role signifying lead or managerial responsibility, but in all cases a role signifying—by definition—some form of authority).
Meta-class template	Templates that inherit common fields from the foundation template.
Policy	A guiding principle; a process constraint, usually at a high level, that focuses on certain aspects of a process and influences the enactment of that process.
Precision	The degree to which the process definition completely specifies all the actions needed to produce accurate results; that is, a precisely defined process, executed with fidelity, produces an accurate result.
Predictability	An indication that the process is intended to terminate and does terminate or that the process is intended to be nonstop and that it does continue until terminated by a control process (or its agent).
Process	A series of actions or operations conducing to an end; a series of actions intended to reach a goal, possibly resulting in products.
Process architecture	A conceptual framework for incorporating process elements in consistent ways (or for signaling that the process element is incompatible with the architecture); a framework within which project-specific processes are defined.

Process control	The external influence over process enactment by other enacting processes. May be driven by process evaluation and may be through control of the process enactment state, reassignment of resources, or change of process goals through process evolution.
Process definition	An instantiation of a process design for a specific project team or individual. Consists of a partially ordered set of process steps that is enactable. Each process step may be refined into more detailed process steps. A process definition may consist of (sub)process definitions that can be concurrently enacted. Process definitions, when enactable by humans, are referred to as *process scripts*. Process definitions for nonhuman enactment are referred to as *process programs*.
Process evolution	The evolution of process definitions (static) as well as the evolution of enacting processes (dynamic), e.g., non-stop processes. Both static and dynamic change must be managed to ensure stability of the process and control over the process results.
Process model	A possibly partial process definition for the purpose of modeling certain characteristics of an actual process. Process models can be analyzed and validated, and, if enactable, simulate the modeled process. Process models may model process architecture, design, project plans, etc. Process models are at times used to predict process behavior.
Process modeling	Extends and constrains process definition by requiring that the process model adhere to a predefined set of objects, relationships, methods, and structural conventions, the last of which are often rendered graphically.
Process representation	The combined or sequential efforts of jointly performing process definition and process modeling.
Process supports	Any non-throughput item that is needed by an activity for the activity to be performed. Activities need products, as that typically is the purpose of activities: to accept one or more products, modify, manipulate, inspect, and possibly create one or more new products,

and pass those along to other activities. However, more is needed by an activity than just the products. These nonproduct items are all modeled as supports. Two common types of support are roles and resources.

Products

The vast majority of artifacts that pass through a process—for example, code modules, end-user guidebooks, circuit boards, and anything else tangibly produced by a process. Products can be decomposed into subproducts, sub-subproducts, etc.

Project

An enactable or enacting process whose architecture has control processes (project management) and enacting processes performing the project tasks.

Project management

An enactable or enacting process whose goal is to create project plans and, when authorized, instantiate them, monitor them, and control their enactment. These responsibilities are commonly known as project planning (i.e., development of process plans) and project control (i.e., process evaluation of plan information and process control to make adjustments, if necessary).

Project manager

A human agent enacting the control process responsible for the execution of a project.

Redundancy

A process task or step that is not required by an error-free enactment. Redundancy thus compensates for human or other errors in process enactment.

Research

A by-product of a process; differs from products in that research is considered intangible. If, for instance, the research leads to a technical paper, that paper is modeled as a product. However, if experiments or investigations are being performed within one or more events but nothing tangible is available as evidence of the work, the throughput can still be explicitly modeled as a research (intangible) artifact. As with products, research can be decomposed into subresearch, sub-subresearch, etc. This decomposition is captured within a model by the inclusion relation.

Resources	Nonhuman items needed to support an event—for example: equipment, office space, supplies, funding. All items that might be required to support an event can be modeled as resources. Resources can be decomposed (using the inclusion relation) so that while one level of event abstraction shows that the training building is required, at a lower or more detailed level of abstraction the support might show that only a small classroom is actually required.
Robustness	The degree to which the process rejects unauthorized process control and/or modification (intrusion).
Role	Individual humans or humans working in concert toward a common goal or set of goals. Consequently, "programmer," "manager," "clerk," etc., all define roles that can be assumed by individuals. "Programming team," "inspection department," and "quality assurance division" also define roles—but organizational roles as opposed to individual ones. For process definition, roles can be defined at all levels of abstractions.
Spiral	One or more cycles.
Subclass template	Templates used to refine and distinguish process information.
Task	A process (step), typically enacted by a human, requiring process planning and control.
Tiers of usage	Tiers that separate process definition work by degree of formality. Tier 1 usage requires the least degree of formality. Tier 4 usage requires a high degree of formality.

REFERENCES

Boehm, B., and F. Belz, 1989: "Experiences with the Spiral Model as a Process Model Generator," In *Proceedings of the 5th International Software Process Workshop,* pp. 43–45.

"CASE and the Management of Risk," 1992. Presented at the CASE World Conference, Santa Monica, California, February 18–20.

Coleman, Glenn L., Charles P. Ellison, Gentry P. Gardner, Daniel L. Sandini, and John W. Brackett, 1990: *Experience in Modeling a Concurrent Software System Using STATEMATE.* Proceedings of the 1990 IEEE International Conference on Computer Systems and Software Engineering, pp. 104–108.

Department of Defense, 1985: *Technical Reviews and Audits for Systems, Requirements, and Computer Programs.* DOD-STD-1521B. Washington, D.C.

Department of Defense, 1988: *Military Standard: Defense System Software Development,* DOD-STD-2167A. Washington, D.C.

Fagan, M. E., 1986: "Advances in Software Inspections." In *IEEE Transactions on Software Engineering,* Volume SE-12, Number 7, pp. 744–751.

Feiler, Peter H., and Watts S. Humphrey, 1992: *Software Process Development and Enactment: Concepts and Definitions.* CMU/SEI-02-TR-4. Pittsburgh: Software Engineering Institute, Carnegie-Mellon University.

Grove, Andrew S., 1983: *High Output Management.* New York: Random House.

Harel, David, 1988: *Statecharts: A Visual Formalism for Complex Systems.* Department of Applied Mathematics, Weizmann Institute of Science, Rehovat, Israel.

Harrington, J., 1987: *The Improvement Process: How America's Leading Companies Improve Quality.* Milwaukee: McGraw-Hill.

Henderson, W., and P. Taylor, 1991: "Embedded Processes in Stochastic Petri Nets." *IEEE Transactions on Software Engineering* 17, 2.

Humphrey, W., 1989: *Managing the Software Process.* Software Engineering Institute Series in Software Engineering. Reading, Mass.: Addison-Wesley.

Implementation Management Associates, 1992: Accelerating Change Workshop. Brighton, Colo.: IMA.

Kellner, M., 1989: "Representation Formalisms for Software Process Modeling." *Proceedings of the 4th International Software Process Workshop.*

Kolman, Bernard, and Robert C. Busby, 1984: *Discrete Mathematical Structures for Computer Science.* Englewood Cliffs, N.J.: Prentice-Hall.

Levis, Alexander, 1992: Class lecture notes during ECE590/SYST659, Spring, George Mason University.

Marca, David A., and Clement L. McGowan, 1988: *SADT: Structured Analysis Design Technique.* New York: McGraw-Hill.

Paulk, Mark, William Curtis, Mary Beth Chrissis, and Charles V. Weber, 1993: *Capability Maturity Model for Software, version 1.1.* CMU/SEI-93-TR-24. Pittsburgh: Software Engineering Institute.

Radice, Ronald A., and Richard W. Phillips, 1988: *Software Engineering: An Industrial Approach.* Englewood Cliffs, N.J.: Prentice-Hall.

Redwine, S. T., 1991: "Process Architecture Issues." In *Proceedings of the Seventh International Software Process Workshop,* Yountville, California, pp. 117-120.

Redwine, S. T., and W. E. Riddle, 1985: "Software Technology Maturation." In *Proceedings of the 8th International Conference on Software Engineering,* IEEE.

Sage, Andrew, 1993: "Systems Engineering for Software Intensive Systems." Presentation by Software Productivity Consortium, September 23.

Sanden, Bo, 1992: *Software Systems Construction: Sequential and Concurrent Designs Implemented in Ada.* Prepublished textbook used at George Mason University, Spring.

Sanden, Bo, 1992: *3.0 Statecharts.* Supplemental Handout #2 for INFT821. George Mason University, Spring.

Singh, Baldev, 1992: *Interaction Roles: A Coordination Model.* CT-084-92. MCC Technical Report.

Singh, Baldev, and Gail L. Rein, 1992: *Role Interaction Nets (RINs): A Process Description Formalism.* CT-083-92. MCC Technical Report.

Software Productivity Consortium, 1992: *Process Definition and Modeling Guidebook.* SPC-92041-CMC, version 01.00.02. Herndon, Va.

Software Productivity Consortium, 1993a: *Managing Process Improvement: A Guidebook for Implementing Change.* SPC-93105-CMC, version 01.00.06. Herndon, Va.

Software Productivity Consortium, 1993b: *Using New Technologies: A Technology Transfer Guidebook.* SPC-92046-CMC, version 02.00.08. Herndon, Va.

Software Productivity Consortium, 1994: *Process Engineering with the Evolutionary Spiral Process Model.* SPC-93089-CMC, version 01.00.06. Herndon, Va.

"A Spiral Model of Software Development and Enhancement," 1986. *ACM Software Engineering Notes* 11:22–42.

"A Spiral Model of Software Development and Enhancement," 1988. *IEEE Computer* 21:61–72.

Venkatraman, N., 1991: "IT-Induced Business Reconfiguration." In *Corporation for the 1990's.* Edited by Michael S. Scott Morton. New York: Oxford University Press.

BIBLIOGRAPHY

Bechtold, R., and Coan, J. "A Database Architecture for Process Engineering and Process Asset Repositories." *Proceedings of the Seventh Annual Software Technology Conference.* Sponsored by the Deparments of the Air Force, Army, and Navy. Salt Lake City, Utah, April, 1995.

Bechtold, R. "Lessons Learned from Developing and Delivering CMM-based Process Improvement Training." *Proceedings of the Sixth Software Engineering Process Group National Meeting.* Dallas, Texas, April, 1994.

Bechtold, R. "Attribute-Driven Knowledge Bases for Intelligent Computer Assisted Training." *Proceedings of the Second Symposium on Artificial Intelligence Applications in Personnel Management.* March, 1994.

Bechtold, R. "Risk Representation and Evaluation in Expert System Logistics Process Models." *Proceedings of the Symposium on Advanced Information Systems & Technology for Acquisition, Logistics & Personnel Management.* March, 1994.

Bechtold, R. "Neural Net Optimization of Personnel Training Programs." *Proceedings of the Second Symposium on Artificial Intelligence Applications in Personnel Management.* March, 1993.

Bechtold, R. "A Rulebase Taxonomy for Integrated Expert System Support of Program Management Processes and Process Improvement." *Proceedings of the Fifth Forum on Artificial Intelligence in Program Management.* March, 1993.

Bechtold, R. "Application of Knowledge Attributes in Process Quality and Productivity Analysis." *Proceedings of the Third Annual Symposium of the International Association of Knowledge Engineers.* November, 1992.

Bechtold, R. "Software Engineering Process Support Based on Fuzzy Imploding Petri Nets." *Proceedings of the ACM 30th Annual Southeast Conference.* April, 1992.

Bechtold, R. "Software Acquisition Risk Mitigation Through Fuzzy Matrix Requirements Specifications." *Proceedings of the Fourth Forum on Artificial Intelligence in Acquisition Management.* April, 1992.

Bechtold, R. "Knowledge Attributes: Fuzzy Application of Temporal Constraints in Active Expert Database Systems." *Proceedings of the IEEE/ACM International Conference on Developing and Managing Expert System Programs.* October, 1991.

Britton, K. H., R. A. Parker, and D. L. Parnas. "A Procedure for Designing Abstract Interfaces for Device Interface Modules." In *Proceedings, 5ICSE,* pp. 195–204, 1981.

Clements, P. C., R. A. Parker, D. L. Parnas, J. E. Shore, and K. H. Britton. *A Standard Organization for Specifying Abstract Interfaces.* NRL Report 8815, June 14, 1984.

Curtis, B. *Modeling, Measuring, and Managing Software Development Process. The M3 Life Boat for Software Tarpits.* Tutorial 4, 13th Internal Conference on Software Engineering, 1991.

Feiler, Peter, and Watts Humphrey. *Software Process Definitions Draft Document.* Pittsburgh: Software Engineering Institute, Carnegie-Mellon University, 1991.

Guindon, R. *A Framework for Building Software Development Environments: System Design as Ill-Structured Problems and as an Opportunistic Process.* MCC Technical Report STP-298-88, 1988.

Kirby, J. Jr., R. C. T. Lai, and D. M. Weiss. "A Formalization of a Design Process." In *Proceedings, 1990 Pacific Northwest Software Quality Conference*, October 29–31, 1990.

Osterweil, L. "Software Processes Are Software Too." In *Proceedings, 9ICSE*. March 1987.

Parnas, D. L. "On the Criteria to Be Used in Decomposing a System into Modules." *Communications of the ACM* 15, 12 (1972): 1053–1058.

Parnas, D. L., and P. C. Clements. "A Rational Design Process: How and Why to Fake It." *IEEE Transactions on Software Engineering,* February 1986.

Potts, C. "A Generic Model for Representing Design Methods." In *Proceedings, 11ICSE*, 1989.

Potts, C., and G. Bruns. "Recording the Reasons for Design Decisions." In *Proceedings, 10ICSE*, April 1988.

Rendes, Barry, and Ralph M. Stair, Jr. *Quantitative Analysis for Management.* 3rd ed. Boston: Allyn and Bacon, 1988.

INDEX